# SOCCER

## $TATE IN THE STATES

By

*Bob Lowe*

ISBN: 978-969-2992-94-7

*Dedicated to the memory of Grant Wahl*

# Table of Contents

# Introduction

When I was a kid, baseball and boxing were the two dominant sports. Football, basketball, horse racing, and hockey were next. Soccer? Not even on the radar.

There are many books about the history of soccer in the United States. There will be references to soccer's rich past in my book; this text is about the here and now.

What is the business of soccer like in America today? What is the difference between the many leagues populating the soccer landscape? How did these teams start? What are various clubs worth from an investor's perspective? How much money do players make?

The one benefit of being dry-docked by orthoscopic knee surgery? I engulfed myself in speed reading soccer books, subscribed to Substacks, listened to podcasts, added streaming subscriptions, scanned the interwebs for all things "fútbol," and planned my Wednesdays and Saturdays around the best games to watch.

I became somewhat of a Method actor, breathing and exhaling soccer 24/7 for six months. Rumor has it I started using phrases like "unlucky," "brilliant," and "bloody right" around the house. Soccer... became my life.

What is the difference between NISA and NPSL? You know about MLS, but what is MLS NEXT vs. MLS NEXT Pro, and why should you care? What's the deal with the USLs? If "League Two," why do they play in level four of the pyramid? The alphabet soup continues with UPSL, and let's not even bring up MASL or the W League, at least for a minute.

Are you a soccer-savant of American soccer? OK, let's talk about Orange County, Calif.: Orange County Soccer Club, the California United Strikers, and the Orange County Football Club. Match them with the proper league: UPSL, NISA, or the USL Championship?

The book will break it down, decode the acronyms, and provide 2022 championship recaps of all leagues, from Division One to Four. Spoiler: The state of soccer in the USA is trending positively.

The "Ted Lasso" television series continues to capture the fancy of many Americans who were ambivalent to—or had disdain for—soccer beforehand. Hollywood actors investing in an international team (Wrexham) also brings the interest in soccer to a new level, another boon for the sport.

As an aside, one aspect of "Ted Lasso" that I love: the show captures the bond that British communities have with their club. And that's a lot of passion: The English Football Association boasts 40,000 teams under its governance. That's not a typo!

Every town has a soccer team. The club may not play in the Premier League, but they are part of the fabric of Britain—with passionate rivalries and the opportunity to move up the ladder if they have a stellar season.

How serious are Europeans about soccer and their team? Check out this clip of a *training session* of Dutch team Ajax, a day before facing a rival side. https://fb.watch/ibSiHQRaJB/

And while we don't yet have this fervor in American soccer, the essence of this book is to honor the thousands of points of light that we do have around the U.S. Each team has a collection of fans, players, and a community that spreads the gospel.

Professional soccer is different than traditional American sports — football, baseball, basketball, and hockey. What other sport has multiple outside competitions during a team's regular-season schedule? Soccer does. A club can play a U.S. Open Cup or CONCACAF Champions League game on Wednesday and must factor that in to prepare for Saturday's traditional league match.

Even though I participated in many sports growing up in sunny California, my soccer career consisted of just a brief stint in elementary school. Soccer in the 1970s had yet to reach the participation boon it would achieve a decade later in the USA.

As a youngster, I devoured the Los Angeles Times sports section daily. I'd buy all the sports books at school book fairs. I even recall purchasing soccer magazines as a kid.

When the Los Angeles Aztecs joined the North American Soccer League (NASL) in 1974, they joined the Dodgers, Lakers, Rams, and UCLA as teams I followed.

The Aztecs advanced over the Miami Toros to win the 1974 NASL title. The match was even at 3-3 after regulation. LA hit all five penalty kicks to prevail, 5-3. This was the first American pro soccer game televised on network television (CBS).

The Aztecs should've hosted this game as they had more points. CBS, however, did not want the contest to be played at the Los Angeles Memorial Coliseum because it would need to be a sellout at the 90,000+ seat stadium to be aired in LA on television. Local blackouts were the norm to protect the home "gate" in the 1970s. The game was sent to Miami. It seems the business of soccer has always reared its head.

The LA Aztecs folded in 1981. Their legacy: Winning one championship and employing two past-their-prime legends: George Best and Johan Cruyff.

I had the opportunity to cover the San Diego Sockers while in college. The Sockers were playing in the NASL's indoor and outdoor circuits. The outdoor league died in 1984, but the Sockers continued their indoor success in the Major Indoor Soccer League (MISL).

The Sockers kept winning and getting good attendance. Yet the team always seemed to be in financial turmoil. Such was the case for soccer in the USA. It was caveat emptor if you wanted to invest in the business of soccer.

The Sockers are alive today; their 2022 team won a championship for the 16th time. They now play in the Major Arena Soccer League (MASL), and their trophy is named after the legendary Sockers' coach, Ron Newman.

How has the business of U.S. Soccer changed? Well, I attended my first USMNT game in 1993. It was a tie vs. Canada in front of 5,700 fans at Orange Coast College in Costa Mesa, Calif. Twenty-nine years later, I witnessed another draw between the two neighbors. More than 40,000 fans watched the 2022 match at Nissan Stadium (an NFL venue) in Nashville.

The United States' participation in World Cup(s) has and will continue to fuel the growth of American soccer. Every league and team expects a bump after the recently concluded 2022 Men's World Cup in Qatar. And just wait until 2026. Soccer at all levels will reap a bonanza when the USA, Canada, and Mexico share World Cup hosting duties.

Everything about American soccer can't be covered within these pages. Collegiate soccer deserves its own book and will not be discussed in-depth here. And while there are teams below level 4 on the American men's and women's soccer pyramids—and they can qualify for the U.S. Open Cup on the men's side—lower amateur leagues won't be noted in detail in this book.

The negatives—hooliganism, riots, alleged bribery, misogyny, player wage issues, harassment, and abuse of athletes—are part of the soccer landscape. These issues are not unique to soccer and cannot be ignored if the game is to reach its potential.

Finally, there will be changes and updates after book publication. New teams, franchises changing leagues, high-profile player acquisitions, and other newsworthy events will occur. And that is part of the appeal of the great dynamic soccer ecosystem.

I hope this book conveys the passion of the players, fans, coaches, and owners that make up the ever-changing nature of this beautiful game, American style.

And globally, who is the greatest soccer player of all time? "Bloody, right" you need to read the book to find out.

"Ole, ole, ole. Ole!"

# PART I.

## THE BACK THIRD

*History, Men's Soccer in the USA*

# 1.

# The USA Soccer Men's Pyramid

T he United States soccer league system is a collection of the country's professional and amateur teams. The system — or pyramid as it's called — is not connected via a promotion and relegation system, unlike in most other nations.

In other words, a team in the second division currently has no opportunity to move up to the first division. MLS/first division teams also have no risk of falling through the "trapdoor" to a lower league.

The United States Soccer Federation (USSF), the national governing body of the sport, defines and sets the standards for men's and women's professional leagues at three levels. The USSF sets minimums for investor financing; market/population requirements; adequate stadiums; staffing; and media demands.

The sport is sanctioned for men and women under the International Federation of Association Football (FIFA). CONCACAF — the Confederation of North American, Central American, and Caribbean Association — governs American soccer at the regional level.

Major League Soccer (MLS) is the lone Division One men's league, and USL Championship (USLC) is the country's only approved second-division operation.

According to USSF numbers, MLS's primary owners need a net worth of $40 million. The investors must be worth $70 million or more. For the USL Championship, a principal owner must have a net worth of $20 million and own at least 35 percent of the club.

There are three men's leagues in the third division: USL League One (yes, this is confusing!), the National Independent Soccer Association (NISA), and MLS NEXT Pro (MLSNP). The minimum requirement set by the USSF for D3 is a net worth of $10 million. The primary investor must own at least 35 percent of the team.

In 2022, there were 107 teams in the top three levels of professional soccer: 28 in MLS; 27 in USLC; 11 in USL1; 10 in the NISA; and 21 for the inaugural season of MLSNP.

In this book, we will also cover the "pre-professional" leagues, too. The leagues are the National Premier Soccer League (NPSL), the USL Division 2 (USL2), and the United Professional Soccer League (UPSL). They are considered fourth division, which is not officially recognized in the pyramid by the USSF.

The higher the league, the more games they play. MLS, for example, plays 34 regular season games. But with the addition of the CONCACAF Champions League, the US Open Cup, and the expanding Leagues Cup (vs. Mexican clubs), the number is higher and varies according to how far each team progresses in the various competitions. It's plausible that the Philadelphia Union may play an astonishing 50 matches in the 2023 calendar year.

The USL Championship plays 32 games and also runs a March to November season. USL League One plays 30 games on a similar calendar.

If you drop down to the fourth level, teams can play as few as ten regular season contests in their truncated summer campaigns. Fourth division teams are technically amateur but often go by the moniker of "pre-professional" and are not sanctioned by the USSF.

Most of the players in Division 4 are current college soccer players. Traditional American sports fans might relate to college wood-bat baseball leagues, most notably the Cape Cod League, as a reference point.

# 2.

# Division One: Major League Soccer and the old NASL

<br>

〜〜〜

A s a condition of FIFA awarding the USA the right to host the 1994 World Cup, the USSF had to pledge to establish a Division One professional men's soccer league. Major League Soccer started in 1996.

No mention of MLS would be complete without discussing the North American Soccer League (NASL) first, which operated from 1968 to 1984. The NASL's golden years occurred in the mid-1970s when Pelé, regarded as the most famous—if not the best—soccer player, came to play with the iconic New York Cosmos.

Pele's immense popularity gave the league a much-needed publicity boost. The Cosmos averaged 3,500 fans in 1974 before Pelé arrived. The next year? The team averaged more than 40,000. The Brazilian icon earned $6 million (about $30 million in 2023) in his three years playing in the NASL.

The problem: acquiring high-priced stars from Europe and South America hurt the league's financial viability. There was only *one* Pelé, and nobody else had his impact.

Additionally, the development of American soccer players was never a goal of the NASL. The league only required two native-born players on every roster. The U.S. Men's Soccer Team, not surprisingly, achieved little success on the global or regional stage during the NASL era.

As NASL struggled near its end, however, the league and the USSF pivoted. Team America was conceived as a professional version of the United States Men's National Team. It played as a league franchise during the 1983 season. The strategy: improve the USMNT in preparation for the 1986 World Cup. The team was based in Washington, D.C., and played its home games at RFK Stadium.

After a promising start, Team America finished in last place (10-20 record) and drew only 13,000 fans per game in its one year of existence. The American men also failed to qualify to reach the World Cup.

View a video of Team America here: https://youtu.be/ntOmm5uLGX4

The MLS was determined *not* to recreate the NASL. Instead, the MLS would operate like a viable business.

Unlike the NASL—or most professional sports leagues, for that matter—MLS acts as a single entity. Instead of operating as a mix of independently owned clubs, MLS teams are managed by "investor owners." This anomaly is unique to MLS since MLB, NBA, NHL, etc., all use a team franchise model.

To illustrate the two ownership models, let's use McDonald's restaurant as an example. Some restaurants are franchises purchased from the Golden Arches. Others are company-owned stores. The latter would be the model used by MLS.

Additionally, MLS—like other professional leagues in the country—has a fixed membership model. Promotion and relegation—or "pro-rel" —is used in most other soccer nations. As such, a select number of teams move up and down the pyramid. Pro-rel is a topic that arouses great passion in the soccer community. It's not likely, however, that the USA will adopt this model in the near future.

The simple reason? Nobody wants to invest $ 300 million in an MLS franchise and then be relegated to a minor league in year two. The system makes sense where soccer has evolved organically elsewhere but not in the 21st Century USA.

In 2023, there are many reasons to believe MLS is on solid financial footing.

-MLS will field 29 teams in 2023, up from just 12 in 2007.

-A handful of cities are lobbying for the coveted 30th MLS franchise.

-A progressive media rights deal (10 years/$2.5B) was cut in 2022.

-Only the NFL and MLB average more than the 21,305-per-game attendance of MLS.

Optimal venues for MLS teams have emerged as a crucial part of the league's business model. There has been a renaissance of "soccer-specific stadiums" in the league. Columbus, which began the renaissance in 1999, is on its *second* fútbol-first park after Lower.com

Field opened in 2021. In 2023, 22 of the 29 teams will be playing in soccer-specific structures.

MLS started with ten teams: Colorado Rapids; Columbus Crew; Dallas Burn; D.C. United; Kansas City Wiz; Los Angeles Galaxy; New England Revolution; New York/New Jersey MetroStars; San Jose Clash; and Tampa Bay Mutiny.

The one outlier/non-major league city? Columbus.

MLS selected Columbus because it had 11,500 season seats pre-ordered by excited soccer fans. The Crew's grassroots beginning, and working-class logo aptly fit the franchise. Columbus tried a rebrand in 2022, but the backlash prevented deep-sixing the Crew name.

Crew owner Anthony Precourt tried to move the franchise to Austin. Instead, new ownership took over the Crew, and the team stayed in Ohio. In 2021 Precourt's new team—Austin FC—began play in MLS.

Actor Matthew McConaughey is a minority of the club. He followed other celebrity owners in MLS: Drew Carey (Seattle) and Will Ferrell (LAFC).

# 3.

# MLS Florida Amputation

Phil West's book "United States of Soccer" summed up MLS's dire situation in 2001: "The simple answer as to what happened comes down to surgical analogy: The MLS was a patient in grave danger, and Florida had to be amputated."

Two Florida teams—the Tampa Bay Mutiny (original franchise) and the Miami Fusion (added in 1997)—were contracted after the 2001 season.

The Mutiny experienced little success on the field or at the gate. We'll never know what would have transpired if Malcolm Glazer had accepted the invitation to purchase the team. Instead, the owner of the NFL's Tampa Bay Buccaneers invested in a soccer team abroad. Glazer bought a stake in a little club called Manchester United. The Glazers are now the controlling owners of a club worth upwards of $3 billion.

After its disappointing start, the Fusion turned things around. Solid management, coaching, and wise player acquisitions dramatically improved the team in the 2001 season. The Fusion won the Supporters' Shield with the best regular-season performance, captured the Eastern Conference title, and advanced to the league semifinals.

Attendance improved as well, but they remained the fourth-worst in the league, with an average of 11,177 fans per match. Owner Ken Horowitz—who paid an astronomical $20 million for the franchise—invested heavily in making Lockhart Stadium a solid soccer-first venue. In order to be financially viable, Horowitz banked on paying crowds of 14,000 to 15,000.

You can't help but compare today's Inter Miami franchise two decades later to the MLS's first team in South Florida. Part-owner David Beckham and his group made a huge splash. A new downtown stadium is planned, but the new club is back at the same (upgraded again) Fort Lauderdale venue, now called DRV Pink Stadium.

Inter Miami CF's stadium plans took a big step forward in April 2022. The Miami City Commission granted a 99-year lease agreement to the club's owners for the Miami Freedom Park project. The plan includes a privately financed 25,000-seat stadium to house the team, nicknamed the Herons. Unfortunately, the shovel often takes years to finally hit the dirt.

Beckham's team appears to be in Fort Lauderdale for a while. The Herons averaged 12,637 fans in the 2022 regular season (down from 13,847 in 2021) at DRV Pink Stadium—close to the Fusion's 14K goal at the start of the century.

Will Inter Miami be in the impressive-looking stadium by 2025? Will the hole in the roof adequately cool off those hot South Florida nights?

Miami is a competitive and fickle sports town. Other South Florida pro teams struggle for fan support, especially the Marlins of MLB.

The good news? Beckham's 2022 team squeaked into the MLS playoffs as the sixth of seven teams in the Eastern Conference. It may be the most impressive achievement in the league, considering the club was under harsh sanctions for violating MLS' salary and roster guidelines during the 2020 season.

# 4.

# The Saviors of MLS

The MLS Cup trophy was named the Philip F. Anschutz Cup in 2008—for a good reason. In 2002, three owners (Bob Kraft, the Hunt family, and Phil Anschutz) owned all 10 MLS clubs. Anschutz owned five at one point.

It's safe to say MLS was on thin ice in the early years. After a promising first season, attendance dropped substantially in every MLS market, except in Washington, D.C. Led by coach Bruce Arena, D.C. United won three of the first four MLS Cups. They also had a 14% increase in attendance in the same period. Winning is good for business.

In the early days, there were not enough American soccer players to adequately outfit the clubs. Famous foreign players such as Jorge Campos, Raul Diaz Arce, Marco Etcheverry, and Carlos Valderrama were needed for their drawing power. And their talent and flair became a feature of MLS's early credibility.

The American stars—fresh names from the 1994 World Cup—were paid well and divvied throughout the league. But the international stars cost the MLS substantially, in both transfer fees and high salaries. The paltry budgets meant the bottom half of every roster had players earning as little as $12,000.

Something had to change.

Don Garber took over as commissioner in 1999. In addition to the stadium-building boom, he took control of television coverage and kept viewership on an upswing. The league invested in talent by paying players more. The teams generated revenue through jersey sponsorships. But perhaps the most significant move was the creation of Soccer United Marketing.

SUM began in 2002 and managed all sponsorship, licensing, and advertising for MLS and other soccer properties in the USA. The most notable and profitable property was the U.S. senior national teams. Additionally, SUM managed the media and marketing rights for its popular games played in the USA.

One hiccup for MLS was the sad legacy of Chivas USA. Chivas began playing in 2005 and had early success. Yet poor management and lack of investment by its Mexican parent club of the same name saw the flailing team average a measly 7,064 fans in its final year. Despite the contraction of Chivas USA, the league simultaneously was actually on a positive trajectory of adding franchises.

MLS took ownership of Chivas for its final MLS campaign. Instead of rebranding the franchise under new ownership and name, the league decided to cut its losses and chloroform the Chivas USA experiment. The Los Angeles Football Club (LAFC) was added in 2018, four years after Chivas closed its doors.

Similar to the grassroots beginning of the Columbus Crew, consider the birth of the Philadelphia Union. The Sons of Ben fan group started before the Union secured an MLS franchise. The supporters showed up at the 2007 MLS Cup at RFK Stadium in Washington, D.C. (Houston defeated New England, 2-1, in the match.) The Sons of Ben were crucial in Philly getting a team in 2008. The Union entered the league in 2010.

MLS grew from 12 to 20 franchises between 2007 and 2015. With each additional club came a franchise fee that augmented the bottom line for the other teams/league.

MLS 2.0—when the league beat extinction—appeared in 2006 or 2007. What changed?

 -Substantial MLS expansion

-The league entered the Canadian market

- David Beckham joined the LA Galaxy

-Designated player rule attracted high-priced stars, exempt from salary cap rules

-Soccer-specific stadium boom aided the profitability of teams

-Focus on player development and academy programs

# 5.

# Soccer Player Development

"It has to be said that the sport is expensive (in the USA), very expensive. For example, in order for my children to play on a good football (soccer) team, I have to pay $3,500 per child. It is not for the figure, but for the whole concept. I dislike it very much because not everyone has the money needed, and the sport should be something for everyone, because it unites people of whatever origin."

Zlatan Ibrahimović, former LA Galaxy striker, December 2020

The most consistent complaint about American soccer is the "pay to play" model for top-level youth travel soccer.

American kids are introduced to the game at the recreational soccer level. After talented players are identified in recreation leagues, they are often steered to expensive year-round programs. A pro career or a college scholarship is the carrot at the end of the stick.

In the early days of Major League Soccer, most American soccer talents played for American universities. As such, the league held its annual "SuperDraft" to parcel out the best soccer players.

A lot has changed in the past 25 years. The SuperDraft is still held, but it now plays a reduced role in assigning talent to MLS rosters. Instead, numerous elite soccer-playing Americans now align with academies and programs in the USA (and abroad) to begin their careers.

When MLS began, only a handful of American men's soccer players competed abroad. Nearly thirty years later? According to YanksAbroad.co, more than 120 Americans played soccer outside of the USA (as of November 2022).

Other than MLS, the vast amount of money in soccer is scattered around the country in youth leagues. Field space rental, transportation, and high-level coaching are not free.

The traditional soccer model outside of the USA works like this: Liam joins the local club in his early teen years. He signs with the hometown club as a pro at 16 or 17. Or, young Liam is sold to a bigger club where he resides with a host family or lives in an academy setting.

MLS is playing catchup. Perhaps Barcelona America setting up an academy in Arizona motivated MLS. And other foreign clubs have taken similar steps to promote their brands and playing style in the USA.

According to Garber, MLS teams collectively spend $100 million annually in their youth development academies. During qualifying for the 2022 World Cup, 17 of the 38 USMNT players came through an MLS academy program.

FC Dallas and its development program have been highly successful. Five of the 26 players on the 2022 USMNT World Cup roster had connections to FCD. Kellyn Acosta, Jesús Ferriera, Weston McKennie, and Shaq Moore are former Dallas Academy players. Walker Zimmerman played with the MLS team. Reggie Cannon and Ricardo Pepi, who didn't make the final World Cup roster, played with the FC Dallas Academy.

Philadelphia opened its YSC Academy in 2013. The Union built a high school, along with its soccer training facilities. Real Salt Lake has a charter school to complement its soccer development program.

No story on player development would be complete without a mention of Project 40, launched in 1997. Now called Generation Adidas, the initiative between MLS and the USSF sought to improve the player pool for the U.S. Men's National Team. The priority: Preparing American players for the 2000 Olympics and the 2010 World Cup—when they would be in their prime.

Since few Americans played abroad and MLS didn't yet have a reserve league or teams, the project made sense. Designed by elite European youth coaches, the "40" denoted the number of annual competitive games needed to play to develop faster. By contrast, the American college soccer season plays about half as many games and wouldn't develop as well.

Each player earned a $24,000 contract, the league minimum at the time. It wasn't much money then and, even with inflation, only amounts to roughly $40,000 in 2023. While that's well below the league's minimum today, the players were provided a five-year academic package. It covered tuition up to $37,500 if the players used the money for college within ten years. This helped mitigate the risk of players abandoning a college scholarship for the pros.

An impressive number of talented players launched their pro careers with Project 40. The program has included the following USMNT players: Freddy Adu; Jozy Altidore; DaMarcus Beasley; Kyle Beckerman; Carlos Bocanegra; Michael Bradley; Clint Dempsey; Maurice Edu; Brad Guzan; Tim Howard; Sacha Kljestan; Ben Olsen; and Nick Rimando.

Each MLS club shared players for the Project 40 teams' weekend games. Interestingly, Project 40 fielded a team in the American Professional Soccer League (APSL) for three seasons: 1998, 1999, and 2000. The APSL was the top minor league in the USA, and the Project 40 club had no home games.

In addition to lousy travel, the young upstarts were resented by their APSL competition. Grown men toiling in APSL felt *they* deserved a shot at MLS, too, and it showed in their energy when facing the hand-picked youngsters. Nevertheless, Project 40 reached the quarterfinals of the APSL playoffs in 1999 and advanced to the third round of the U.S. Open Cup in the team's final campaign in 2000.

The high cost of travel was the main reason Project 40 left APSL play. The team was sent on European and South American tours and played well against some of the world's top reserve units. The program lives on today—not as a standalone squad but within the confines of MLS clubs—as a way for players to matriculate to the pros while paving the way for a future college degree.

One funny story regarding Project 40 came from one of its coaches: Lothar Osiander. The roster varied each week. Osiander was astounded after he was supplied a team with all left-footed players for one weekend.

For more on the history of Project 40, read here: https://tinyurl.com/yhr6rr2p

# 6.

# What's in a Name?

If you weren't paying attention when MLS started, there were some curious names and brands. Does anybody miss the Burn, Clash, MetroStars, or Wiz? Did you recall that the New York/New Jersey MetroStars had a yellow taxicab as its logo?

The nicknames, logos, and brands seemed to be marketed to a skateboard/soccer/street ball demographic that did not exist.

MLS, however, began to embrace global soccer norms. Regular-season games could end in a tie. The clock was switched to international standards (counting up, not down). It did away with its quirky 35-yard shootouts.

And these 35-yard shootouts were both ridiculous and compelling at the same time! Watch here:

https://www.youtube.com/watch?v=pNExAtWu0CU

DC United was certainly ahead of the curve in terms of early team success and its Europa-like soccer name. Later, other squads began adopting monikers familiar in Europe, such as FC, City, Sporting, and Real. They also began using their city or state's name.

Teams that take on a geographic name—like Atlanta United or Minnesota United, for example —often use secondary monikers like the Five Stripes and Loons, respectively.

Another cool thing about MLS nicknames? Four franchises use names dating back to the NASL: the Portland Timbers; San Jose Earthquakes; Seattle Sounders; and the Vancouver Whitecaps.

It's a shame the Cosmos or Rowdies haven't resurfaced in MLS, but they live on in lower-league clubs in NYC and Tampa, respectively.

A few current and former monikers that deserve acclaim include Racing Louisville (clever); Rochester Raging Rhinos (brash); Colorado Caribou (hip); Indy Eleven (unique), and Bethlehem Steel (historical).

While it made sense that none of the original cities kept the NASL names, the league now has a peculiar mix of nicknames. NASL throwbacks, original MLS tags, and traditional soccer names such as City, United, FC, Real, Inter, Sporting, and SC.

One outlier: the Red Bulls.

The Red Bulls are the only MLS team with a corporate name. The company's philosophy is to use soccer clubs to create brand awareness and beverage sales. Other than the Harrison, N.J.-based MLS side, Red Bull-owned first-division football clubs include Austria's RB Salzburg, RB Leipzig of Germany, and Brazil's RB Bragantino.

One last point on team names: best practices include a reference to your geographic area. In the NWSL, for example, most folks can figure out that Angel City is Los Angeles and Gotham is in New York.

However, when I see "OL Reign," my first impression is Orlando, not Seattle. OL's name is from its parent company: Olympique Lyonnais of the French Women's League.

# 7.

# MLS Salaries and Franchise Values

S t. Louis FC—which begins play in 2023—paid $200 million to join MLS. That total is 500% more than the cost of an expansion franchise ten years ago. In 2019, the Charlotte FC franchise fee paid by billionaire David Tepper was a cool $325 million.

In January 2023, Forbes listed the value of the Los Angeles Football Club at $1 billion.

For player salaries, MLS Designated player Carlos Vela of LAFC and the LA Galaxy's Javier "Chicharito" Hernandez earn more than $7 million per season. Italian Lorenzo Insigne was the highest-paid MLS player. The Toronto FC forward had a cap hit of $14 million for the 2022 season.

The designated player rule began with British star David Beckham. The "Beckham Rule" was implemented when the international icon joined MLS and the LA Galaxy in 2007. In 2015, to entice more talented players to join MLS, the league added targeted allocation money (TAM).

According to a 2022 MLS player survey, the average player salary was $514,720, approximately $100K higher than the previous season. The survey, published by Spotrac, indicated that 99 athletes made $1 million or more.

Team salaries in the same survey ranged from $9.7 million to more than $32 million.

As many as 20 players on an MLS roster counted against the club's 2022 salary budget of $4,900,000. They are referred to as the club's "senior roster." There are no limits on how many Americans can fill out a roster. The same is true with the three Canadian teams. There are no limits on native-born players playing for MLS clubs.

MLS has 224 international roster slots divided among the 28 MLS clubs (in 2022), which averages eight per team. These slots are tradable. Some squads may have more than eight, and other clubs may have fewer on their roster.

The league does offer a "homegrown" option that rewards a club for developing and promoting players in its area. The rule allows MLS clubs to sign local players to academies and then transfer them to the senior team. Homegrown players do not count against the league's salary cap.

## 2022 MLS Team payrolls

*Team Payroll in U.S. Dollars*

Toronto $32,234,728

LA Galaxy $27,303,314

Miami $24,194,278

Atlanta $22,431,357

Chicago $19,355,763

LAFC $19,001,888

New England $18,584,553

Columbus $17,892,808

Seattle $16,983,746

Houston $16,867,485

New York City $16,504,148

DC United $16,282,352

Cincinnati $16,281,087

Dallas $15,761,683

Vancouver $14,897,149

Kansas City $14,736,204

Austin $14,639,786

Salt Lake $14,609,198

Nashville $14,145,780

Montreal $13,059,176

Orlando $11,956,012

Charlotte $11,661,661

Portland $11,377,505

Minnesota $11,157,156

San Jose $10,702,272

Colorado $10,570,955

Philadelphia $10,360,287

New York Red Bulls $9,642,386

*Source: The Blue Testament*

# MLS 15 Best-paid players

*guaranteed compensation*

1. Lorenzo Insigne, Toronto, $14 million

2. Xherdan Shaqiri, Chicago, $8.153 million

3. Javier 'Chicharito' Hernandez, Galaxy, $7.443 million

4. Federico Bernardeschi, Toronto, $6.256 million

5. Douglas Costa, Galaxy, $5.8 million

6. Gonzalo Higuain, Miami, $5.794 million

7. Hector Herrera, Houston, $5.247 million

8. Alejandro Pozuelo, Miami, $4.693 million

9. Luiz Araujo, Atlanta, $4,480 million

10. Jozy Altidore*, New England, 4,265 million

11. Christian Benteke, D.C. United, $4.183 million

12. Josef Martinez, Atlanta, $4,142 million

13. Lucas Zelarayan, Columbus, $3.7 million

14. Carles Gil, New England, 3.546 million

15. Rodolfo Pizarro#, Miami, $3.35 million

*-Altidore is on loan to Puebla of Liga MX*

*#-Pizarro is on loan to Monterrey of Liga MX*

# 8.

# Soccer Transfer Market

E ach sport and league have its own unique form of player development, but the word "transfer" is tied to global football. Soccer clubs typically sponsor youth programs advancing up to the senior team. In general, nobody can be a professional in soccer until the age of 16.

How does a transfer work? Here's an example of a transfer in the United Kingdom. Liam, a talented youth player, is identified and signed early with fifth-division Wrexham AFC. He does well. Wrexham sells him to second-division Swansea for $5 million.

Savvy soccer minds often put a "sell-on" clause when transferring a player. A sell-on is when the seller gets a future cut if the player is sold down the road. This means Wrexham would get a cut—let's say 25%—if Swansea sells Liam on to Chelsea for $20 million.

Wrexham reaps a bounty from that sell-on. They get double their initial transfer price. And Swansea profits by holding and developing a player now sought by a global super club. And, let's face it, Super Clubs have money to burn,

FIFA reported that $7.8 billion was spent on soccer player transfers in 2019. Due to the Covid pandemic, the number of global transfers and total fees decreased. In 2021 the number was $4.6 billion; MLS claimed $159 million in transfer fees that same year.

The largest transfer fee (as of January 2023) was for the Brazilian star Neymar. He moved from Barcelona to Paris St. Germain of France's Ligue 1 in 2017. His transfer fee eclipsed $240 million. Neymar's 2019 salary was more than $100 million—making him the third highest-paid footballer behind Lionel Messi and Cristiano Ronaldo.

Meanwhile, American Christian Pulisic transferred from Borussia Dortmund in Germany to English club Chelsea in 2019 for $67 million. Spotrac—which has an extensive list of salary and transfer projections for footballers—listed his salary in 2022 and 2023 at $9.4 million.

Brenden Aaronson's initial transfer out of Philadelphia Union is now among MLS's most expensive outbound deals. The initial fee was $6.5 million from RB Salzburg. After Aaronson moved from Salzburg to Leeds for $30 million, the Union cashed in again due to its "sell-on clause."

With savvy management, the transfer market can be the gift that keeps on giving. And FC Dallas is cashing in on the market.

In 2022, the $20-million fee for Ricardo Pepi set a then-record for an American player transferring to foreign soil at FC Augsburg. Defender Bryan Reynolds was sold to AS Roma from FC Dallas in 2021. That transfer fee was $8.5 million and included incentives and a sell-on clause.

Instead of transferring Jesús Ferreira, FC Dallas made him its designated player. He was one of four Americans to be a DP in the 2022 season, joining Gyasi Zardes (Colorado), Darlington Nagbe (Columbus), and Walker Zimmerman (Nashville SC).

Born in Colombia—to a soccer-playing father—Ferreira moved to Texas at age 10. He signed a "homegrown contract" with FC Dallas in 2016. He inked a four-year contract with FCD in 2019 but then earned the DP status—and a $2-million annual salary—before the 2022 season.

FC Dallas now has the reputation of being a tremendous creator and seller of talent. The team has moved Cannon, Pepi, Chris Richards, and Tanner Tessman for $40 million in transfer fees. It's one way to do business, but fans of the team were irked at seeing their budding young players sold off without acquiring players in return.

For followers of Major League Baseball, the best comparison may be the Tampa Bay Rays. The organization is notorious for unloading developed talent at peak value. The Rays pawn off their stars before they have to pay them the big bucks and receive more affordable prospects in return.

The small-market Rays have been impressively competitive with their business model. Time will tell for FC Dallas. And remember that with single-entity ownership in MLS, transfer fees are shared with the league.

Transfers, however, are not relegated to just MLS teams. After winning the USL Championship in 2021, The Orange County Soccer Club sold successfully on the transfer market. They transferred

Ronaldo Damus—a Haitian international who was the MVP for its title run—to Swedish club Sundsvall for a six-figure fee in March 2022. OCSC sent Kobi Henry to Reims two months later for a USLC record of $700,000. Henry signed a five-year contract with the French club.

No matter the sport, salary caps—luxury taxes, and other impediments to big spending—exist. Most fans want their teams to be creative and find ways to field quality clubs that compete for championships.

Does a high payroll result in winning? In some cases, yes.

In a graph listed in the book "Soccernomics," the high payrolls in the English Premier League from 2011 to 2020 were Manchester City, Manchester United, Chelsea, Liverpool, and Arsenal. They were also the five most successful teams in the period.

By contrast, expensive team payrolls have had mixed results in MLS. In 2022 high-priced Toronto FC didn't make the playoffs, while frugal Philadelphia advanced to the MLS Cup Final.

# 9.

# 2022 Playoffs and MLS Cup

In the MLS Western Conference Final, the Los Angeles Football Club defeated Austin FC, 3-0. The Supporters' Shield winners dominated their Texas foes before a raucous home crowd. LAFC led in shots (22-7) and corner kicks (11-5).

Cristian "Chicho" Arango scored in the 29th minute. The Black and Gold got the gift of an own goal in the 62nd minute. The visitors did not get a shot on goal until the 80th minute. Kwadwo Opoku tallied the match's last score one minute later.

The Eastern Conference final between home-standing Philadelphia and defending champion NYCFC was a more competitive match. The Union prevailed, 3-1. Following a scoreless first half, Maxi Moralez netted a goal for the visitors in the 57th minute.

But the Union, in front of its passionate crowd, responded promptly. Julián Carranza got the equalizer in the 60th minute off a free-kick pass from Jakob Glesnes. Dániel Gazdag (67th minute) and Cory Burke (76th minute) recorded the other two goals.

NYCFC led in shots (13-10) and had possession for 65 percent of the match.

The 2022 MLS Cup featured the top two regular-season finishers for the first time since 2003. LAFC from the Western Conference and its Eastern Conference foe: the Philadelphia Union.

The Black and Gold's 22,000-seat home stadium seemed a little too cozy for this affair when the game could've attracted at least double that amount at another venue.

After two overtime periods, LAFC won the match on penalty kicks after the teams battled to a 3-3 draw. They became the eighth team to win the Supporters' Shield and MLS Cup in the same year.

And if there was a pregame MVP? Your money would not have been on backup LA goalkeeper John McCarthy. The backstop was exceptional in the shootout. Interestingly, the 30-year-old journeyman grew up in Philly, attended La Salle, and played four seasons with the Union.

Dan Gazdag missed badly on the Union's first PK. McCarthy then saved the next two attempts on Jose Martinez and Kai Wagner to lift the home team to the title. LAFC got PK conversions from Denis Bouanga, Ryan Hollingshead, and Ilie Sánchez for the win.

"A dream come true," McCarthy told the LA Times following the match. "It still doesn't make sense, doesn't add up."

Why was McCarthy in the position to be the hero? Starting LAFC goalkeeper Maxime Crepeau was dealt a red card (the second in MLS Cup history) in the 116th minute after coming out of the box to challenge a serious Union scoring chance. That foul may have saved the victory, but Crepeau left the game on a stretcher.

Fox Sports and its broadcasters extolled the match as the best MLS Cup Final, if not the best MLS match in history. It could be up for debate, but no viewer was cheated.

Kellyn Acosta put LA on the board in the 28th minute after his free kick deflected into the goal. The Union tied the match in the 59th minute after Gazdag scored off a pass from Martinez.

LAFC captain Carlos Vela hit a corner kick that Jesús Murillo headed in for the 2-1 edge. It was the 83rd minute, but Philly responded two minutes later as Jack Elliott tied the match off a free kick by Wagner.

The visitors got another tally from Elliott in the fourth minute of extra time. But a bench player who could not break the vaunted LAFC lineup, Gareth Bale, sent the match to PKs. His brilliant header off a crossing pass from Diego Palacios in the eighth minute of stoppage time in the second overtime period (the latest goal in MLS Cup history) extended the match.

Bale was one of the many high-priced acquisitions (LA doubled the Union's $9 million payroll) LAFC made during the season. The Black and Gold won, but the Welsh star rarely left the bench during their late regular-season and playoff run.

The teams were tied in points during the regular season, and LA won the hosting due to a tiebreaker. The match stats indicated the visitors led in shots (17-16), possession (53-47), and corners (5-4).

And even though it seemed like Philadelphia was the team of destiny, it was LA who stepped forward in penalty kicks. Bale and LAFC were happy to hand the plaudits over to McCarthy for his heroics.

Prescient Fox commentator Stuart Holden noted that McCarthy could be inserted into the game for a penalty shootout. A few minutes later, Crepeau's serious leg injury occurred, and the backup keeper entered the game.

The broadcast team had a great shot of Philly Coach Jim Curtin looking at his watch and yelling to his team to hold on for "four minutes" of the extra time for the win. Bale's goal, however, happened two minutes later.

Perhaps Jeff Rueter's headline for his story in The Athletic summed up the game best: "Gareth Bale, the backup goalkeeper, and the greatest ever MLS Cup."

The Los Angeles Football Club created the 3252 supporters' section in its home: BMO Stadium. The raucous crowds at LAFC home games produce one of the best game-day atmospheres in MLS. (Photograph by the author.)

# 10.

# United Soccer League

The United Soccer League (USL) claims to be the largest and fastest-growing professional soccer organization in North America. USL oversees the Championship (USSF Division II); League One (USSF Division III); League Two (pre-Professional men); W League (pre-professional women); USL Academy (pre-professional); and Super Y League (youth).

Based in Tampa, Fla., the USL has grown during the past decade. It features a staff of more than 100 professionals across 18 departments ranging from operations, digital, communications, and club services, providing support to member clubs and outside partners.

Jake Edwards is the president of USL. The English-bred Edwards moved to the USA and played prep soccer in New Jersey. He later played collegiately at James Madison University before making 250 appearances in a professional career abroad and in the USA.

Edwards played three seasons (1998-2000) for the now-heralded Wrexham AFC before returning to the States. He had a short playing stint with DC United in 2001 and later signed with the Charleston Battery of the A League. He returned to the UK as a player.

43

Before Edwards's retirement as a player, he also served as the commercial manager for his final club: the Solihull Moors FC. He increased on-field advertising by 50 percent and sourced the club's first stadium naming rights sponsorship. During that time, Edwards earned an MBA from Warwick Business School and became an executive at London-based consulting firm Octagon Worldwide.

In 2013, Edwards joined the USL front office as they launched a strategic 10-year plan to grow the league. One goal was to increase the professional side from beyond ten teams. They've already succeeded. Its Championship and League One fielded 38 squads combined in 2022. USL also sought to devise a business model that would be sustainable and appeal to investors.

In September 2022, USL announced a partnership with the Caribbean Football Union. The CFU is a subsidiary of CONCACAF, with 31 member nations. The wide-ranging agreement seeks to offer more professional opportunities for players, coaches, referees, and administrative staff in the USLC and League One.

"Caribbean football has made tremendous contributions to the USL over the years," said Edwards in a press release. "This partnership creates an exciting opportunity to augment that legacy. We are thrilled to work with the Caribbean Football Union and its members to grow the sport throughout the region and impact our communities together."

Scores of foreign players (including many from the Caribbean) already compete in American leagues, from MLS to Division 4. With the new partnership, USL will aid Caribbean leagues and clubs with best practices to implement in their homelands.

In November 2022, USL announced an expected collective bargaining agreement with the players' association for League One (third division). This followed an earlier agreement reached with players of the USL Championship (second division).

# 11.

# USL Championship (Division 2)

The United Soccer League Championship was started in 2011 and earned second-division status from the USSF in 2017.

USLC began with the required minimum of 12 teams in 2011. The Charleston Battery and the Pittsburgh Riverhounds are the only two teams to play every year of the Championship.

Reserve/second teams from MLS boosted the league as the Championship grew from 14 teams in 2014 to 29 squads in 2016. The MLS farm teams filled out the standings in the USLC, but their objectives didn't mesh.

USLC teams are looking to build solid teams/businesses in a viable second division league. The MLS second squads, however, prioritized player development and were/are a feeder for the major league side.

Prior to joining MLS, Orlando City SC captured three regular-season crowns. They are tied with Louisville City FC for two championships—the most in league history.

Along with Orlando, Cincinnati, Montreal, and Nashville used their success in the USL Championship to springboard to MLS. The

Vancouver Whitecaps, Portland Timbers, and Seattle Sounders used earlier minor league iterations of USL to launch their first-division futures.

FC Cincinnati (FCC) had an impressive run on the pitch and at the gate before moving to MLS. FCC had a handful of crowds surpassing 20,000 fans, two times over 30,000, including the league record on September 29, 2018, of 31,478 versus Indy Eleven.

Buoyed by FCC, USLC set a regular season average attendance record of 4,923 and a playoff mark of 7,786 in 2018. The league has held steady by attracting more than 4K in the regular season every year since and averaged 6,645 for the 2021 postseason.

Louisville City (12,000+) and New Mexico United (10,000+) were the shining stars of USLC fandom in 2022. For 2023, shedding the MLS farm teams will significantly help the Championship's attendance average.

As for media, the Championship has a contract with ESPN that puts all games on the ESPN+ streaming platform. Additionally, 18 other matches are televised on the linear services owned by ESPN/ABC.

The Championship also has a broadcast deal with OneFootball in Italy and FloSports for the Caribbean. The Caribbean connection is a natural fit due to the symbiotic relationship between the USL and the CFU.

In recent years, the darling in minor league soccer has been Detroit City FC, a USLC member since 2022. DCFC played in the National Premier Soccer League from 2012 to 2019 and the National Independent Soccer Association in 2020 and 2021. The team defeated the visiting Los Angeles Force, 1-0, before 7,231 Motor City fans to cap the 2021 NISA campaign. DCFC then joined USLC for the 2022 season.

Detroit City FC is a great story in part because it was started as a grassroots effort launched by locals. Its website boasts: "Detroit City FC has developed into a minor league soccer success story, with one of the most exciting match atmospheres in North America, consistently sold-out games, and passionate supporters."

It's hard to dispute that statement. Detroit City plays its home matches at historic Keyworth Stadium in Hamtramck, an enclave of Detroit. Fans and volunteers helped refurbish the local landmark—an attractive-looking venue streamed on ESPN+ for league or U.S. Open Cup matches.

In another story of lore: "the seed of DCFC was planted in 2010, on the soccer pitch at Belle Isle in downtown Detroit. That grass—the very same that was transported from the Pontiac Silverdome after the 1994 World Cup—was the original home of the Detroit City Fútbol League (DCFL), a co-ed, recreational league that pitted players from teams representing the many historic neighborhoods of Detroit."

Inspired by the success of recreation soccer in Detroit, DCFL founder Sean Mann pitched four friends an idea to further tap into the growing interest in the sport by founding a minor league soccer team to play in downtown Detroit. The rest is history.

The Championship is strategically positioned in large USA cities that don't have an MLS franchise and, in most cases, have a population of at least one million people. The league boasts teams in major league markets like San Antonio, San Diego, Sacramento, Phoenix, Indianapolis, Memphis, Oklahoma City, Oakland, Pittsburgh, and Tampa.

The rest of the league is in mostly minor league municipalities, with easily accessible transportation options. The one outlier is the Rio Grande Valley Toros. Their Edinburg, Texas home is off the beaten path and quite the trek from major airports and a formidable road trip for visiting clubs.

The USL Championship will soon welcome teams in Des Moines, Iowa, Milwaukee and Queens, N.Y. Queensboro already fields a youth team and USL W League entries.

USL Championship Playoffs: The Championship semifinals saw Louisville City edge the visiting Tampa Bay Rowdies, 1-0. Homestanding San Antonio FC dispatched the Colorado Springs Switchbacks FC, 2-0.

Like the MLS Championship the weekend earlier, the USLC final pitted the league's two best clubs. Louisville, the top finishers in the East, traveled to Texas for the championship match. SAFC won the Supporters' Shield with 77 points. LFC netted 72 in the regular season.

Played before a sold-out crowd of 8,000 at Toyota Park, Santiago Patino tallied twice as SAFC won, 3-1.

Patino, the match MVP, converted a penalty kick just before halftime. Samuel Adrenian, on loan from the Seattle Sounders, put the home team ahead 2-0 in the 63rd minute on a header. Six minutes later, Patino, a Colombia native who played at Florida International, knocked one in from about 12 yards out.

Brian Ownby put Louisville on the scoreboard in the 78th minute.

The championship was the first for SAFC—which the NBA's San Antonio Spurs own.

# 12.

# USL League One (Division 3)

U SL League One targets municipalities of 150,000 or more. According to the USL website: "League One has focused on launching new clubs in markets that possess strong local ownership groups, populations with broad-based diversity, a vibrant millennial and strong family base, established corporate support, and stadiums to properly showcase the sport for fans, partners and the public. "

Spokane, Wash. is a city that could appeal to several different leagues. Perhaps an MLSNP team for the Seattle Sounders FC? Could the USL Championship be a fit?

Nope. A USL League One and a USL W League team plan to occupy a new stadium in downtown Spokane. The 5,000-seat public stadium will also host local and high school events and games.

Spokane joins fellow debutantes Santa Barbara (Calif.) Sky FC in 2024 as USL One expansion teams.

In 2023, two teams come on board: One Knox (Knoxville, Tenn.) and the Lexington (Ky.) Sporting Club. The new additions will boost USL One to 12 teams for the season.

Expansion and strategic growth are crucial to the financial viability of each club. More teams added can increase regional play, reduce travel costs and create geographic rivalries. For example, the new Santa Barbara and Spokane sides will make join Fresno as the only teams on the West coast.

Another West Coast team—FC Tucson—dropped down to USL League 2 in 2023 but could resurface as it seeks a proper stadium to meet League One standards.

The 2022 campaign was the fourth season of League One play. Previous champions were North Texas FC (2019), Greenville Triumph SC (2020), and Union Omaha (2021).

The collective bargaining agreement between League One and the players is the first for any Division 3 league worldwide. The groundbreaking deal guarantees players a minimum salary of $2,000 per month. When the agreement ends in 2027, the 10-month salary increases to $2,500. For more details, please see the story on Backheeled.com: https://tinyurl.com/4wv5ydak

USL League One Playoffs and Championship: Six teams qualified for the USL One playoffs in 2022. After the 30-game regular season, the Richmond Kickers (51 points) and the Greenville Triumph (46 points) earned byes to advance to the semifinal round.

Union Omaha, the defending champion and League One darling from its play in the U.S. Open Cup, had its run come to an end. They lost at the Chattanooga Red Wolves, 1-0, in one quarterfinal match. In the other game, home-standing South Georgia Tormenta edged the Charlotte Independence, 2-1.

The semifinal round pitted Chattanooga at Richmond and saw South Georgia visit Greenville. Both visitors prevailed by 1-0 scores, setting up a Chattanooga-South Georgia finale. Richmond became the first regular-season champion to fail to win the championship trophy.

In the championship match, broadcast live on ESPN 2, Jamil Roberts pounded home a left-footed shot in the 82nd minute as the South Georgia Tormenta edged the Chattanooga Red Wolves, 2-1, on Nov. 6, 2022.

Kazaiah Sterling assisted an open Roberts, who was left open on the far side. Roberts entered the match as a substitute in the 78th minute. Sterling had the game's first goal. He converted a PK in the 35th minute.

In the third minute of first-half stoppage time, Chattanooga tied the match. On a free kick, Jose Carrera-Garcia delivered a ball that Alex Tejera headed home.

Roberts and Sterling are both Englishmen. After the match, Roberts indicated the goal and championship were the biggest soccer achievement in his life. That's quite a statement since he also scored the game-winning goal when Marshall University won the 2021 NCAA College Cup.

Sterling, who netted four of South Georgia's goals in the postseason, was the championship match MVP.

South Georgia was the fourth league champion in League One's fourth year of existence.

The Tormenta play in the smallest market in USL pro soccer. The match was just their fourth game played in their new stadium, which is only partially completed. Match attendance was 3,045.

The championship was the second for South Georgia this year. Their USL W League women captured a title earlier in the summer.

# 13.

# National Independent Soccer Association (Division 3)

~~~~~

The National Independent Soccer Association debuted in 2019. The league initially played a fall-to-spring season, paralleling many leagues around the globe. NISA now plays the traditional American schedule (spring to fall).

NISA seeks to be the leader of independent club soccer in the USA. NISA touts its "club-first" model compared to the stricter top-led structure of the nation's top two competitors: MLS and the USL.

Post-pandemic, NISA listed four clubs as "on hiatus" for the 2022 campaign: a stark reminder of the financial realities many minor league teams face.

In recent years, the league lost Detroit FC (2020 and 2021 champions), the Oakland Roots, and Miami FC to the USL Championship. The loss of the Detroit side, often mentioned as the crown jewel of lower-level soccer, was a particularly tough blow for NISA.

Many NISA teams began as amateur sides—often with complementary youth programs—before adding a professional team. NISA's Independent Cup and NISA Nation league underscore its commitment and strong ties to top amateur teams. As such, NISA has contacts with clubs that may be ready and recruited to join its D3 professional league.

NISA offers "solidarity payments" to amateur teams after a professional spot in NISA is taken by a player. These pseudo-transfers build goodwill the amateur clubs. Additionally, NISA is considering a promotion-relegation dynamic within its league, but no date or concrete plan is in place.

In the minor league soccer community, a few organizations pop up as franchises that have "killed it."

Chattanooga FC, of NISA, is on that elite list.

Before joining the NISA, CFC played in the National Premier Soccer League. The club had a phenomenal run in NPSL, winning eight conference titles in 11 years. CFC reached four league finals and qualified for six U.S. Open Cups.

Chattanooga FC—playing home games at Finley Stadium on the campus of UT Chattanooga—boasted the highest average and single-game attendance in the NPSL. In its inaugural match on May 16, 2009, over 1,600 fans watched Chattanooga FC host Atlanta FC. The crowds kept growing. On July 26, 2014, the team set a league attendance record of 8,878 for their playoff against the Sacramento Gold. In 2015, 18,227 fans came to the Finley Stadium for the match between

Chattanooga FC and New York Cosmos B. It became a U.S. fourth-tier attendance record.

It was no surprise that CFC was ready to move up a level—but that was not without challenges.

If a competitor tries to steal a top executive and grab your home venue (Finley Stadium), you must be doing something right. Those problems started when the Chattanooga Red Wolves formed in 2018. The Red Wolves even attempted a takeover of Chattanooga's youth academy.

But CFC and its supporters fought back. In 2019—in grassroots rebellion fashion—the club became the first to offer ownership shares to the public (that Green Bay Packers model) and crowdfunded. CFC raised more than $870,000 and now boasts owners from all over the world. Chattanooga was first slated to play in a new NPSL pro league. That league didn't materialize, and CFC instead joined NISA.

The Red Wolves (USL One) and CFC now share the Scenic City. Fun fact: Chattanooga FC's predominant supporters' group is known as the "Chattahooligans."

A team closing shop during the season is a very bad look. In August 2022, NISA was dealt a blow: Bay Cities FC of Redwood City, Calif. dropped out due to financial reasons. That left the Western Conference with just three teams: Albion, Cal United, and the LA Force. Valley United FC (Mesa, Ariz.) was scheduled to start the year with NISA but backed out, leaving the league with nine teams to begin the 2022 year.

NISA plans for growth, grooming successful amateur sides to compete in the D3 pro level, might be flawed. Did NISA clubs meet the suggested financial requirements for Division 3, as stated by the USSF? In early 2023, reports were that the Federation was indeed concerned about the status of a few NISA clubs.

It's the nature of the USA pyramid beast in the USA soccer pyramid to have movement between leagues. From 2020 to 2022, however, NISA lost four clubs to other leagues. Three teams left for the USL Championship.

As for player movement, a dozen or more NISA players have moved on from the league. Most have appeared in USL League One, but a few are vying for spots in USLC rosters.

In early 2023 the buzz about NISA and its ability to have another season was in question. Protagonist Soccer reported that the league had only a few solid organizations ready for the upcoming season. One bad sign: league officials were owed $10,000 in unpaid fees from 2022.

Nevertheless, NISA announced it would resume with nine teams playing in a single table format. Three new teams Club de Lyon FC (Orlando, Fla.), Gold Star FC (Mich.), and the Savannah (Ga.) Clovers join the league in 2023.

The six returning clubs are Albion San Diego; Chattanooga FC; Los Angeles Force; Maryland Bobcats FC; Michigan Bobcats; and City Union, a merger of Flower (Rochester, N.Y.) and Salt City Union (Syracuse, N.Y.). The combined club will play in both New York municipalities.

2022 Playoffs and Championship: Cal United and Chattanooga earned the first-round byes in the six-team playoff field. Both clubs won 14 matches, and the two teams were the only clubs to average more than two goals per game in the regular season.

In the quarterfinal round, the Michigan Stars FC defeated the Syracuse Pulse, and Albion San Diego bested the Maryland Bobcats. The home teams won by a 2-0 result in both games.

In the semifinals, the top-seeded Strikers hosted Southern California rival Albion. In the other match, the Michigan Stars traveled to Chattanooga. Albion upset the Strikers (4-2) while visiting Michigan upended the Red Stars (1-0).

Anthony Bowie scored the only goal as the Michigan Stars defeated visiting Albion San Diego, 1-0, in the NISA Championship match. The game was played at Romeo High School, north of Detroit, in front of a club-record 1,178 fans.

Bowie, who played collegiately at Western Michigan University, headed in a corner kick in the 31st minute off a pass from Steven Juncaj.

The Stars have plans to build their own soccer-specific stadium. The club was founded in 1982 and used to play in the NPSL before joining NISA in 2019.

# 14.

# MLS NEXT Pro (Division 3)

T he launch of Major League Soccer NEXT Pro in 2022 is perhaps the most significant change to the professional soccer landscape in years. MLS has substantial resources its new league will dramatically alter the dynamics of minor league soccer.

MLS sees NEXT Pro as a bridge between their youth academies and first teams. All MLS clubs with reserve teams in USL Championship or USL League One will move to NEXT Pro in 2023. Before its teams played in USL, MLS tried its own Reserve League from 2005 to 2014.

NEXT Pro began with 21 teams in 2022. All but one franchise— Rochester, N.Y. FC—was affiliated with a Major League Soccer franchise.

The Columbus Crew 2 earned 55 points in the 24-game regular season. They won both the inaugural Supporters' Shield and the MLSNP Cup.

Eight teams made the inaugural playoffs, with four from each conference. Rochester City captured the fourth and final postseason berth in the East. The Crew 2 had a +40-goal differential and won the Cup with a 4-1 win over St. Louis City SC 2.

Jacen Russell-Rowe of Columbus earned the golden boot with 21 goals and also was tabbed the league's most valuable player. Romeo Beckham, the son of David, tied for the MLSNP lead in assists with 10 for Inter Miami FC II. (Romeo was subsequently loaned to England side Brentford.)

MLS's new contract with Apple TV will feature all MLSNP contests as part of the new streaming rights deal.

It's no surprise—with its connection to MLS—that NEXT Pro has a clean and professional website with top-notch graphics. Yet MLSNP also experimented with automated video streaming. The cameras are operated by artificial intelligence rather than humans.

This new resulted in both fan frustration and humor. In one unforgettable instance—in the Scottish League—AI mistook a linesman's bald head for the soccer ball. In that case, the camera followed the linesman's skull—not the ball—or the activity on the field.

See the video here:

https://www.youtube.com/watch?v=i_p5wLoCCiw

MLSNP is akin to AAA baseball in terms of its relation to the major league parent team. Teams from and competing leagues are jockeying for optimal facilities and fan bases. Some minor league teams play in the same city or metropolitan area as the MLS club.

For example, the City of High Point, N.C. approved plans to upgrade and retrofit Truist Point, primarily a baseball stadium for the Atlantic League's High Point Rockers. The Carolina Core FC will begin competition there in 2024 as an independent club, like Rochester. Soccer Hall of Famer Eddie Pope will be the club's chief sporting officer. The High Point native is a three-time MLS Cup Champion and a three-time FIFA World Cup participant.

During its introductory press conference, the Core strategically called out the major soccer youth programs in Central North Carolina. The organization likely sees developing and selling soccer players as a crucial part of its business model.

Near the end of 2022, a third independent MLS NEXT Pro was announced for Cleveland, Ohio. Cleveland is a major league city.

Some MLS clubs will extend their brand footprint and reach outside of their immediate municipality. Nashville's MLSNP team will be based in Huntsville, Ala. In 2023, Huntsville will be the only MLS farm team to play outside a parent market under its own image and likeness. Likely it won't be the last.

Nashville SC owns and operates Huntsville City FC. It views this city, two-hours south of Nashville, as the place to spread its brand and wings.

The City of Huntsville had been looking at soccer as a tenant for its Joe Davis Stadium, a former baseball park that underwent an $8M renovation. The stadium is now a multi-purpose facility that seats 10,488, with 15 air-conditioned skyboxes.

2022 MLSNP Championship: The Columbus Crew II capped an epic first year with a 4-1 win over St. Louis City SC II in the inaugural Major League Soccer NEXT Pro Cup. The match was played on October 8, 2022, before 7,446 fans at Lower.com Field in Columbus.

Isaiah Parente converted a penalty kick in the 45th minute. Marco Micaletto tallied in the third minute of first-half extra time for the 2-0 halftime margin for the Crew 2.

Jean Russell-Rowe added a penalty kick goal in the 58th minute before St. Louis scored. Celio Pompeu netted an 80th minute goal for the visitors. Ryan Telfer closed the game by scoring for Columbus in the 83rd minute.

Both teams collected ten shots in the championship match.

The Carolina Core FC will be one of at least three independent teams in MLS NEXT Pro. High Point, N.C. native son Eddie Pope (pictured) was hired to build a top-notch team in the fledgling league. (Photograph by the author.)

# 15.

# National Premier Soccer League (Division 4)

~~~~~~~~~~~

ounded in 2003, the National Premier Soccer League (NPSL) is a pre-professional league. The league's motto is "A National League with a Regional Focus." The league fielded 92 teams in 2022.

In November 2022, the NPSL was designated by the United States Adult Soccer Association (USASA) as tier 1, the top level of soccer within the USASA.

Dennis Crowley co-founded the Four Square platform and other tech ventures and started the Kingston Stockade team in 2015. He searched for details on launching a team and found nothing. The Stockade, however, still began play the following year in NPSL.

The Stockade hails from Kingston, N.Y (population: 24,000)., which is in the Hudson Valley. The town was founded by Dutch immigrants who built a wooden fortification for the city, which became known as the "stockade district."

It's safe to say that Crowley did not have Gladwell's 10,000 hours of experience as a sports team owner.

The Stockade, a 501c3 non-profit corporation, is a leader in the "open source soccer" movement, which brings transparency and data to building lower-level soccer clubs. Crowley has an updated blog that covers club operations (finances, attendance, streaming, etc.). It can be accessed here: https://www.stockadefc.com/opensourcesoccer

Non-profits are not able to pay their players, which means some teams would need a new business plan or LLC to move to Division 3. Fourth division players maintain their collegiate eligibility, too.

In the Stockade's first year, they paid a one-time $12,500 expansion fee to NPSL (later increased to 15K and then 18.5K). Crowley expected first-year operating costs of $50,000 but ended up spending $80K. The team averaged 750 fans for home games, which was the best in their conference. At the end of the season, Stockade FC still posted a financial loss of about $18K.

By year two, Stockade FC qualified for the prestigious U.S. Open Cup. They beat the organization's goal by two seasons. In extra time, the Stockade lost at the USL 2 member Long Island Roughriders, 6-3.

Check out this video package about Crowley and Stockade FC: https://vimeo.com/178928507

Always the entrepreneur, Crowley launched a mobile application called Street FC. The app allows folks to meet up for pickup soccer games. Street FC also allows players to rate each other and is operational in a handful of urban areas.

# 16.

# A Look Inside: Appalachian FC

Jason O'Keefe turning a negative into a positive: that would be an understatement.

O'Keefe arrived at Appalachian State University in 2016 after stints coaching at some of the nation's most successful men's soccer programs, including North Carolina, Saint Louis, and Wake Forest.

Following two five-win seasons, O'Keefe led ASU to an 8-6-3 record. In 2019, he took the program to great heights after posting 11 wins—the most for the Mountaineers since 2002. App State's defeat of UNC was their first since 1980; it marked the second straight season the Mountaineers beat a ranked team (No. 22 Coastal Carolina in 2018).

Then the bombshell hit. Due to finances within the ASU athletic department, the Mountaineers' men's soccer program would be axed.

"I was devastated for all of us," O'Keefe said. "I didn't know if I would coach college soccer again."

O'Keefe then pivoted with perhaps the perfect business partner to start Appalachian FC. Michael Hitchcock is a former general manager of FC Dallas of MLS. As far back as 1998, he worked in MLS with DC

United, the Colorado Rapids, and the LA Galaxy. He started Playbook Management in 2009.

Bullish on minor league soccer, Hitchcock has ownership in 10 soccer teams around the globe and now six clubs in NPSL. In addition to App FC, he is part owner in Lubbock and Fort Worth, Texas; Napa, Calif.; and Chattanooga, Tenn. But he isn't stopping there. In July 2022, Hitchcock announced a new ownership group in Annapolis, Md. Naptown's owners include former Major League Soccer stars Kyle Beckerman and Alex Yi, both from the Annapolis area.

App FC hit the ground running. Finding a seal, nickname, and mascot was priority one. They hit a home run—or a hat trick—with their sasquatch mascot. The club now has the passionate support of bigfoot and sasquatch enthusiasts worldwide.

This is not a joke. The Boone, N.C. club reached about $150,000 in merchandise sales, eclipsing most of the other top-selling clubs by $75,000.

Appalachian FC has a clean, professional website and uses top-notch graphics for social media. They are one of the few minor league teams to have a standalone "Squatchy" team store that is open year-round.

After merchandise sales, sponsorship/partnerships are the organization's second-best money-maker. App FC's third-best revenue source is ticket sales. They offer premium season ticket packages that provide perks to its most dedicated fans.

App FC also offered limited ownership opportunities via Wefundme. The project raised $78,476 from 217 investors (Green Bay Packers model). According to O'Keefe, the crowd-funded owners have a vote on their board, and there is equity in the investment. This model is becoming popular in many communities. In addition to the cash infusion, your most loyal fans being "owners" can't be measured in dollars alone.

When referencing Hitchcock and his multiple investments, one can't help but think of MLS. Remember the early days when Phillip Anschutz and the Hunt family-owned multiple teams at a time? These well-heeled owners help keep the league afloat. And they understand the potential of soccer as a business in America.

Appalachian FC is fueled by collegiate athletes but features 3-4 locals who have earned spots on the team. One excellent side story for the club? A handful of O'Keefe's former players—who continued their careers at other colleges—returned to Boone to play for the team.

The club qualified for the 2023 U.S. Open Cup. And while this competition is the season highlight for most minor league teams, it creates a challenge for fourth-division clubs that rely on college athletes. For Division 4, the U.S. Open Cup begins in March. The collegiate players don't report until late April. "We will have special tryouts and probably have two distinct teams for 2023," said O'Keefe.

Oh, and O'Keefe did return to NCAA Division I men's soccer. He completed two years leading Robert Morris University near Pittsburgh before resigning in November 2022. He returned to North Carolina and now works in sports management. And team owner O'Keefe is happy to be close to Boone.

Team owners often strike gold. In addition to succeeding on the pitch, Appalachian FC picked sasquatch as a mascot and now has a global following. (Photograph courtesy Appalachian FC.)

*To see when Bigfoot came out of the woods with a soccer ball, view this video: https://www.youtube.com/watch?v=GG1FvNj_Pow*

**2022 NPSL Championship**: In the NPSL finale, FC Motown beat visiting Crossfire Redmond (also known as FX) of Washington state, 4-3, before 2,065 fans at Montclair State University.

Motown usually plays at Drew University. The championship match was moved to MSU, also home to the Red Bulls II. The home club jumped out to a 2-0 lead before FX rallied with three straight goals.

Handy Coby Jean Rodriguez recorded his second goal of the match in the 90th minute to secure the championship for Motown. Ryan Peterson and Franco Catania also scored for the national champs.

"I'm so proud of my team and how we fought just to get to this match," Rodriguez told NPSL.com after the game. "We never got down on ourselves, even when things got tough. We have a lot of fight in our squad, and that's how we've been able to play all season."

FC Motown had quite a year for a Division 4 squad. Nine NPSL sides earned spots in the U.S. Open Cup. FCM qualified for the 2022 Open Cup based on its 2021 campaign (7-2-1 record/defeating Monmouth, 2-0 in the conference playoff final).

Motown earned two straight wins in the 2022 U.S. Open Cup after defeating Westchester United and AC Syracuse Pulse by 1-0 results. In the third round, they tied the new Rochester NYFC team 2-2 after regulation. The MLSNP side, however, advanced over the NPSL team, 4-3, in penalty kicks in a third-round match.

Crossfire Redmond had a mediocre 4-1-5 regular season record in its Pacific Conference. Yet FX caught fire in the playoffs. They had an impressive 3-0 win over the Muskegon Risers in the national semifinal.

In the championship match, the Redmond-based club rebounded from the 3-0 deficit by notching three goals between the 43rd and 49th minutes. Goals by Christian Soto Rincon, Scott Menzies, and Hamza Haddadi were not enough.

# 17.

# USL League Two (Division 4)

Other than MLS, another league thrived after the 1994 World Cup: USL League 2.

In 1995, the United States Interregional Soccer League changed its name to the United States International Soccer League and split into two leagues. One of those leagues ultimately became the USL Second Division.

The Second Division changed its name to the Premier Development League in 1997 before taking on the League 2 moniker in 2019 to align with the USL hierarchy. Yet, the league hasn't changed much and is the country's oldest men's "pre-professional" league.

As mentioned before, a good comparison to League Two—and other fourth-division leagues—would be baseball's summer wood-bat/collegiate baseball leagues.

Rosters consist primarily of collegiate players. Coaches come from colleges throughout the nation for a "Sumner job." Players often stay with "host families," offering savings on expenses and—in many cases—a great experience for both sides. Soccer clubs and leagues have followed this model.

In League Two, nearly every athlete is a returning college soccer player or a recent graduate. USL 2 strives to remain the top pre-professional league in North America (USA and Canada). League Two franchises boast that they provide the opportunity to train and compete at the highest level while maintaining their collegiate eligibility.

In 2022, League Two fielded 113 teams in 16 divisions across four conferences. About two-thirds of the players are currently on collegiate rosters. Roughly two-thirds are Americans. The League also boasts more than 70 players who later earned caps with the U.S. Men's National Team. The current expansion fee in USL 2 is about $50K.

Players can't be paid to play in USL 2, but that doesn't mean former professional players cannot play in the league. Take the example of Danny Szetela.

A New Jersey native, Szetela played at the prestigious IMG Sports Academy as a prep. He was part of the Project 40 Initiative and represented youth and the senior U.S. Men's National Teams (three caps). The midfielder later played in the MLS with the Columbus Crew and DC United.

The 2021 season was the second year Szetela (age 34) was on the Morris Elite Soccer Club roster. The value of such a decorated player can be positive for his college-age teammates.

But Szetela was not the first luminary to play in the league. After retiring and moving to the United States in 2003, Jurgen Klinsmann played for the Orange County Blue Star. A club official listed

Klinsmann on the team sheet to avoid media attention as "Jay Goppingen." The heralded German striker would later coach the U.S. Men's National Team.

**USL 2 Championship Match**: Home-standing Ventura County (Calif.) Fusion defeated the Long Island Rough Riders, 2-1.

Marley Edwards netted the game-winner in the 85th minute for the Fusion. Nathaniel Opoku, who scored the Fusion's first goal, was named match MVP.

Opoku—a native of Ghana—played his freshman year at Lindsey Wilson College, an NAIA institution.

The contest was scoreless at the halftime break. The second half provided a much different dynamic as both sides displayed impressive chances.

Winger Jayden Reid then tallied for Long Island on a combination play. A few minutes later, Opoku converted a bicycle kick right over the head of Long Island keeper Wessel Speel. The match was equal until the 85th minute.

With just minutes to go, Sergio Villalpando found Edwards in space in the penalty area. Edwards hit a low shot to the left corner of the goal, giving Ventura County the game-winner.

The win was the ninth straight for the Fusion. Ventura County last won the USL 2 crown in 2009.

Ventura County finished second in the Southwest Division with an 8-2-2 record and entered the 32-team tournament as the fifth seed in the Western Conference. The Rough Riders, who featured East Coast college players (many from nationally-ranked Hofstra), advanced to the title game after winning the Eastern Conference with a record of 15-1-2.

In the Fall, Opoku transferred to NCAA Division I Syracuse. He scored 11 goals, dished eight assists, and helped the Orange to an NCAA championship—where he was tournament MVP. In January 2023, Opoku signed a contract with British club Leicester City. He began his pro career on loan in Belgium.

# 18.

# A Look Inside: Lionsbridge Football Club

<br>

W hen Mike Vest was a kid, he followed his hometown soccer team: the Kansas City Comets. He dreamed he was one of the team's stars, maybe Gino Schiraldi or Dale Mitchell. His friend was Jan "Goose" Goosens.

Vest went on to have a career in athletic communications and management. But his interest in soccer never dimmed. In fact, it piqued when he read the late, great Grant Wahl's soccer article in October 2016's issue of Sports Illustrated. The story was about the formation of Dennis Crowley's Kingston Stockade.

By 2017, Vest had co-founded the Lionsbridge Football Club. Grant Wahl, who tragically died while covering the 2022 World Cup, changed the landscape of American soccer and, to some extent, the trajectory of Vest's professional life.

Named after an iconic landmark, Lionbridge has had tremendous success in its brief Newport News, Va. existence. The club was voted the 2019 USL Team of the Year; Lionbridge set attendance records for both League Two and all professional soccer teams in Virginia.

"We started as a group of professionals who emphasized community spirit, family entertainment, and local flavor," Vest said. "We wanted the community to be involved from the outset. We sought their feedback choosing our jerseys and even picking our crest."

In 2022 Lionsbridge had an undefeated regular season. They won the Chesapeake Division and, based on their record, earned the USL 2 regular-season title.

Earlier in the season, LFC defeated Peninsula rival Virginia Beach, 2-1, before 3,546 fans on the campus of Christopher Newport University. A free sandwich promotion from a local fast-food chain undoubtedly helped the large crowd.

"We're trying to create a great experience and memories for our fans," said Vest. "I received a message from a season ticket holder. He said his son and friend want to play for Lionsbridge when they are old enough. That's everything to us."

Lionbridge streamed its home games on Facebook, and a few matches appeared on local television. LFC placed a high priority on building community through social media.

Vest considers Lionsbridge "club neutral" as the team does not offer competitive youth programs. Vest believes this choice is ideal for his club to reach all local soccer players and youth programs.

In 2022, Lionsbridge offered six summer camp programs where players can make some pocket change. It's a great way for the team to get out in the community. And good publicity is good business.

Lionsbridge runs a lean business operation. Vest is the only full-time employee. Part-timers and volunteers come on board during the summer season. Vest keeps busy in the off-season by securing and retaining sponsors, keeping fans engaged via social media, and getting ready for January team tryouts.

It's not uncommon for teams to do a press release or a graphic when a player signs a pro contract. LFC promotes its interns—just like they do with their players—when they advance in their careers.

Lionsbridge was second in USL 2 attendance. They trailed only the Des Moines Menace. The Menace are one of the most successful teams in league history. Established in 1995, the club won the national championships in 2004 and 2021 and garnered regular-season titles four times (2002, 2014, 2018, 2019).

The Menace offers a website chock full of its extensive history. Its team roster highlights the colleges/universities, or last club, of its players—which is a tremendous point of interest for many fans. Hall of Famer Laurie Callaway—a player in NASL and manager of MLS's San Jose Clash (1996-97)—had two stints as the coach of the Menace.

The Menace will join the USL Championship in 2024 when its 6,300-capacity stadium—part of a $535-million downtown development—opens for business.

Lionsbridge FC in Newport News, Va., has had impressive success on the field and at the gate. One reason? They steadfastly appeal to cultivate a bond with young people and families in their community. (Photograph courtesy Lionsbridge FC.)

# 19.

# A Look Inside: Minneapolis City SC

L ike Dennis Crowley, Dan Hoedeman of the Minneapolis City Soccer Club is one of those open-book team owners.

Established in 2016, the "Crows" wanted to recreate the local feeling of the Minnesota Thunder's early days. As such, every player is a Minnesota resident. The club is owned by "members" who make critical decisions for the team. These invested owners have had a voice in team colors, logo, and budget.

Their team's motto: "Majorly Fun Minor Soccer." The club is known for its irreverence, a creative Twitter feed (@mplscitysc), and wacky fans. The Crows feature an independent, active, and loud fan group called the "Citizens."

MPLS SC began to play in the Premier League of America, an amateur circuit now part of UPSL's Midwest Division. In 2017, MPLS City SC joined the National Premier Soccer League. The next year the Crows won the NPSL North Conference title and went undefeated in conference play. They followed up with two more consecutive crowns in 2019 and 2021. (There was no 2020 season due to Covid).

In 2022, the Crows became one of the few clubs to sponsor teams in both the USL 2 and the NPSL. The USL 2 team went 1-9-2, and the separate NPSL unit finished 7-6-1.

"We tripped up when we played in both leagues," Hoedeman said. "We underperformed with both sides, so we're looking to 'make it right.' Next year (2023), we will focus on just building the best USL 2 team we can, and with our same Minnesota-centric focus, sort of like Athletic Bilbao of the north." (Note: The La Liga club Bilbao fills its roster exclusively from Spain's Basque region.)

Hoedeman's marketing background shows. The team partnered with European-based street artists to produce guerilla-style murals across their home city. MPLS SC established one of the first amateur club retail stores in the United States; Each year the club releases new "must-have" kits.

The Crows—donning the starkest and boldest color scheme of black and white—play home games in front of a regularly full house at Augsburg University's Edor Nelson Field (1500 capacity) in Minneapolis.

A good logo and branding are vital in marketing any sports team. The Minneapolis City Soccer Club promotes fun and irreverence to its followers. The Crows also have a strong logo and a brilliant color scheme: black and white, which they wear at home. Why hasn't anyone else done this? (Logo from MPLS SC.)

# 20.

# United Premier Soccer League
# (Division 4)

~~~~~~

F ounded in 2011, the United Premier Soccer League is North America's largest men's pro-development soccer league. The UPSL started in Santa Ana, Calif., with just ten teams, and now boasts 400 squads nationwide. Its Premier Division for Spring 2022 had 255 clubs competing for 32 places in its national playoff tournament.

The UPSL features players with origins from 90 different nations participating. More than 50% of players and coaches are of Hispanic descent.

Promotion and relegation is challenging—if not impossible—to implement in the United States at this time. But let's give it up for the plucky UPSL for trying pro-rel. The league announced it would begin a promotion/relegation system starting in 2017. Teams compete in Pro Premier (Division 4) and Championship (Division 5).

Unlike most other D4 leagues, the UPSL plays year-round. After their Spring season commences in August, UPSL begins play for its Fall league in the following month.

2022 UPSL Championship: The Orange County (Calif.) Football Club defeated Beaman United (Tenn.), 3-1, at the historic Columbus Crew Stadium on August 7, 2022.

Cody Shelton had a hat trick for the Southern California club. His third goal in the 82nd minute secured the victory. USMNT legend Paul Caligiuri coaches OCFC.

The championship was the second for Southern California level four soccer programs in two days. The Ventura County Fusion won its second-ever league title after defeating the visiting Long Island Roughriders, 2-1.

The USL 2 and NPSL championships were played at small venues. The UPSL, however, does things differently. The league staged its final four games at the heralded 19,000-seat soccer-specific stadium.

# 21.

# The Hank Steinbrecher Cup

~~~~~~~

T he Hank Steinbrecher Cup is an all-champions tournament that began in 2013. Its name honors Hank Steinbrecher, a National Soccer Hall of Fame member, former Secretary General of the USSF, coach, player, and sports executive.

The annual competition pits the reigning Steinbrecher winner against three champions from three leagues: National Amateur Cup; the NPSL; and USL 2.

Previous winners of the Hank Steinbrecher Cup include Carolina Dynamo, 2013; RWB Adria, 2014; Chattanooga FC, 2015; Chicago Fire U23, 2016; Michigan Bucks, 2017; Michigan Bucks, 2018; and Flint City Bucks, 2019.

2022 Steinbrecher Cup Championship: The Flint City Bucks won their fourth straight Steinbrecher Cup after edging the Denton Diablos of the NPSL, 2-1, on June 5, 2022. It was the first cup contested since 2019 due to the Covid pandemic.

Flint City, representing USL 2, hosted the weekend tournament. The first half was scoreless. The Bucks opened the scoring when Januik Videbaek put back a rebound off the crossbar. The home team notched the eventual game-winner on a header from Daniel Hernandez. Brayan Padilla converted a PK for Denton's goal.

In the semifinals, Flint City defeated Houston Regals, the USSA National Champion, 4-2. In the other semi, Denton beat Lansdowne Yonkers FC—the National Amateur Cup champion—by a 4-2 tally.

# 22.

# The Lamar Hunt U.S. Open Cup

*"The important thing in life is not the triumph but the struggle; the essential thing is not to have conquered but to have fought well."*

*-Pierre de Coubertin, founder of the modern Olympic games*

The Lamar Hunt U.S. Open Cup, also known as the U.S. Open Cup, is a knockout tournament competition in men's American soccer. It is the oldest ongoing national soccer competition in the USA.

The tournament was first held during the 1913–14 season as the National Challenge Cup, with Brooklyn Field Club winning the trophy. The competition was renamed and dedicated to NASL and MLS executive Lamar Hunt by the United States Soccer Federation in 1999.

The American knockout tournament was modeled after the FA Cup. First played during the 1871–72 season, the British tourney is the oldest national football competition in the world.

True to its name, The U.S. Open Cup—which primarily runs from March to September, concurrent with the American soccer calendar— is open to professional and amateur teams throughout the nation.

Clubs below level 4, however, actually start qualifying in the Fall of the previous year.

The tournament champion earns $300,000 in prize money and a berth in the CONCACAF Champions League. The runner-up receives $100,000. The furthest-advancing team from each lower-division league gets $25,000.

The best explanation of the U.S. Open Cup for non-soccer fans would be NCAA March Madness. The thrill of underfunded underdogs defeating those from a higher level is dubbed a "cupset."

MLS sides have dominated the competition since the league began in 1996. No lower division team has won the competition since the Rochester Raging Rhinos in 1999. No minor league club had reached the final since 2008 (Charleston Battery) until Sacramento Republic FC did so in 2022.

Insiders also regard the Lamar Hunt U.S. Open Cup as the least-appreciated property in soccer, if not all American sports. The competition has flown under the radar for many years. U.S. Soccer, however, has ramped up marketing and promotion of the Cup in recent years.

Perhaps the best move was to put all Cup matches (until the championship) available on streaming platforms. Early-round games can be viewed on YouTube. ESPN+ then picks up the games, which usually are on Wednesday evenings. They've also added a live "whip-around" show to check in on all the current matches.

In the early rounds, you get a good look at soccer venues used across the USA. Some sites don't have what we'd call a "stadium" but more of a recreation field appearance. And then there are the hundreds of high school, college, and municipal stadiums that teams call home.

2022 Lamar Hunt U.S. Open Cup Final: There wouldn't be a cupset in the 2022 Lamar Hunt U.S. Open Cup Championship. Orlando City FC of MLS scored three late goals to defeat visiting Sacramento Republic, 3-0, on Sept. 6, 2022.

Facundo Torres had two goals and one assist for the Lions. Torres scored in the 75th minute, in the 80th minute on a penalty kick, and assisted Benji Michel in the 96th minute.

The trophy was the first ever for Orlando.

The Cinderella story for Sacramento ended, but not until the USL Championship side upended three straight MLS teams: San Jose Earthquakes, the LA Galaxy, and Sporting Kansas City.

Orlando City was the stronger club. They outshot the Republic, 15-5.

With a budget of about 10 percent of its MLS opponent, Sacramento hung on for 72 minutes. They managed two shots on goal.

# PART II.

## MIDDLE THIRD

*Fans, Stadiums, National Teams and the*

*Women's Game*

# 23.

# American Fan/Supporter

T he soccer team and the fan have a special relationship. Anyone new to the sport will be struck by what happens after the game. The players and coaches make a point to cheer for the *spectators* following the contest. It's really a special ritual. You'll see it at youth-level soccer to top professional leagues.

There's also an adage in soccer: There are fans, and then there are *supporters.*

Supporters don't just watch the games on television. They attend the games. Supporters are season ticket holders. They might even travel to their club's away games. And in many cases, they make up the unique culture of supporters' sections.

Advice: sit amongst the infamous "3252" for an LAFC game. There are no seats in the section, just handrails for standing. The 3252 is located behind the north goal in the beautiful BMO Stadium. The venue is just steps from the LA Coliseum and sits on the former site of the LA Sports Arena.

The 3252 (named for the number of fans the section holds) fills up early on game day. The drumbeat begins, and the 30 or so flag wavers fill out the section. Before the game, the rhythmic chants begin.

"Dale, dale, dale, black and gold!

Dale, dale, dale, black and gold!

Dah-ley… black gold!"

*Experience the real deal here (and expect these chants to stay in your head for days!): https://tinyurl.com/4y8ethza*

The 3252 has its own membership club, separate from LAFC. It's an all-volunteer unit. Their website is https://the3252.net, where you can join the club, learn the chants, and get involved.

It's not a passive group. There are leaders on the field leading chants. Each section has another sub-leader—known as a "capo" —who revs up the crowd with his/her back to the pitch. The flag wavers get the best workout in the stadium, save for the competing athletes.

Standing in the 3252 requires a bit of sacrifice. One is expected to chant. Learn the damn chants! Those flags do come with obstructed views that move, unlike a permanent beam in Fenway Park, for example. But the video screens offer relief.

And when a goal is scored by the home team? The beer, water, and soda shower mix rains down from above. Be advised that this shower happens even when goals are later overturned by offsides.

The Charlotte Football Club, a 2022 MLS expansion team, placed a high priority on engaging its fan base. In its first home game, an MLS record crowd of 74,479 saw the home team fall to the LA Galaxy, 1-0.

Charlotte FC deploys a "Fan Experience Department" and a full-time job as "chief fan officer."

And then there are the louder fans, both at the games and online. There are opinionated keyboard warrior fans who consume a lot of soccer. The word "trash" is often used to describe a poor performance by a multimillionaire world-class athlete or manager. As evidenced by social media posts, call-in shows, and letters to editors, these folks can be quite critical.

Was Klinsmann fired at the right time? What about Berhalter: When did you get off the Gregg train? How many forwards should the USA have on its roster, and which ones? If Berhalter led the USA to World's biggest prize, many would still want him sacked the next day.

You get the idea.

On a more positive note, the diehard USA fan is dedicated to the national teams. They travel all over the country, wearing patriotic scarves, jerseys, and face paint. They range from kids to senior citizens and include many families.

Sam's Army (as in Uncle Sam) was the unofficial supporters' group for the United States Men's National team from 1995 to 2010. In 2010 there were more than 14,000 members of Sam's Army.

The American Outlaws are now the dominant supporter group for U.S. Soccer. Like Sam's Army, they dress patriotically and usually stand behind a goal during a United States home match. Like an MLS supporters' section, expect to sing and chant throughout the match.

The Outlaws—who support both the men's and women's national teams—boast more than 30,000 members in more than 200 chapters nationwide.

Often, the hardcore fan is dialed into soccer overseas. They might have a favorite English Premier League team or digs La Liga (Spain) or Serie A (Italy)—a preference likely passed down from a parent or grandparent.

Finally, there's another American fan. He or she may hold an American passport but don't expect them to root for the USA—at least against Mexico. The Mexican men's national team—known as El Tri—has had a massive following in the United States for decades. (Note: El Tri refers to the *three* colors on its flag: red, white, and green.)

When it comes to USA-Mexico, the loyalty question can be a difficult one for families and even players. There are many talented young athletes who meet the qualifications to play for the Yanks or El Tri. The choice can be a gut-wrenching decision for such a player.

One might expect that patriotism is the main factor in selecting a nation to play for. Anecdotal evidence suggests, however, it's usually the best opportunity for playing time that clinches the deal.

One other nuance of the soccer supporter—American or not? He/she is a walking billboard. Soccer jerseys started the trend of featuring a sponsor more prominently than the team's name or city. Airlines, automakers, herbal supplements, health care providers, and power tool manufacturers are a sampling of MLS jersey sponsors.

The Philadelphia Union had the name of its kit sponsor—BIMBO—plastered across its jersey in large lettering. That caused a stir. While the name could be seen as a derogatory term by some, BIMBO *is* a legitimate Mexican bread producer.

# 24.

# Venues and the Soccer-Specific Stadium

$\sim\!\sim\!\sim$

I t was a game-changer when Crew Stadium opened in 1999. The Crew played its first three years in Ohio State's famous Horseshoe.

Additionally, the Ohio capital city became the first municipality to open its *second* fútbol-first park after Lower.com Field opened in 2021. In 2023, 22 of MLS 29 teams will be playing in soccer-specific venues.

The soccer-specific stadiums are/were crucial in two areas. First, the smaller stadiums result in a better game day experience for teams and fans. Secondly, MLS teams own or control the facilities, which results in better revenue. Charging others (concerts, for example) is a better business model than renting.

With hindsight, however, the 1999 Crew Stadium is a traditional American bowl-style/American football venue that just happened to house a soccer team. Crew Stadium served a great purpose. It hosted historic USMNT wins over Mexico and lasted for two decades.

The Galaxy was next. They constructed what is now Dignity Health Park in 2003. The stadium—which seats 27,000—boasts the traditional European soccer stadium feel: rectangular architecture and overhangs, which shade fans during contests.

Today's stadiums also have standing sections—with handrails for its most vocal supporters—often located behind a goal. And did we mention constructing new soccer venues in downtown districts? This planning helps city centers and aids local businesses. As for the fan, pre-game meetups at the local brewpub and perhaps a post-match dinner at a restaurant improve the game-day experience.

There are stadiums built or under construction for USL teams, too. In fact, USL is mandating soccer-specific venues for all of its second and third-division squads.

Another huge sign of progress occurred in October 2021 in the National Women's Soccer League. The Kansas City Current unveiled plans for a $70 million privately financed riverfront facility—the first stadium purpose-built for an NWSL team. The structure will hold 11,000 fans and debuts in the 2024 season.

The New England Revolution, a charter member of MLS, still plays in cavernous Gillette Stadium. They average 19,000 in a 66,000-seat NFL venue, which isn't ideal for MLS regular-season play. This makes for a poor experience for the paying public.

Robert Kraft, the wealthy owner of the Revs, could certainly do better. A soccer-specific venue would likely be a better experience for players, fans, and the New England community.

On the other hand, NFL stadiums *do* serve a purpose. Rivalry matches often get moved to places where attendance can double to 50,000 or more for select MLS contests. When a popular European or South American club visits in their preseason during the summer, they regularly fill large venues in the USA.

Additionally, FIFA covets modern NFL stadiums because they offer amenities for fans, corporate partners, and teams. All American stadiums chosen for the 2026 World Cup are NFL venues.

And then there's the elephant in the room: Yankee Stadium and the New York City Football Club.

NYCFC is operated by the deep-pocketed Football Group (of Manchester City fame). It was awarded the franchise in the Big Apple with the expectation that ownership would build a stadium for the team.

The New York Yankees own 20 percent of NYCFC. The novelty of playing at historic Yankee Stadium wore off years ago. The pitch is too narrow. Sharing a field that is predominantly a baseball diamond (the seasons are concurrent), NYCFC played a home playoff game in 2022 at another baseball park: the Mets' Citi Field. The club has also played "home" games in Harrison, N.J., and even Los Angeles.

A much-anticipated announcement finally came days before the 2022 World Cup: NYCFC reached a deal for a stadium in the city. The 25,000-seat facility will be built on a city-owned site in Willets Point in Queens. The $780 million venue will be privately financed but will get public funding in the form of infrastructure for the area.

The stadium will be part of a new complex with a hotel and 2500 housing units. The venue will join two other nearby Queens sports landmarks: The Met's Citi Field and the Billie Jean King Tennis Facility, host of the annual U.S. Open Tennis tournament. NYCFC's stadium is slated to open for the 2027 season.

Queensboro FC, which shares the Big Apple with NYCFC, has announced a 7,500-seat venue designed by Populous for its USLC, W League, and youth squads. It will be ready for the 2023 campaign.

# 25.

# Give Me a Sign

Savvy teams and owners know the value of signage. The sidelines across from the television broadcast prime real estate. In the lower leagues, signs from sponsors adorn the area.

LED signage is a huge revenue source for clubs. Newer stadiums and those in MLS and other leagues use LED signs. This type of sign allows for both dynamic ad rotation and time-sensitive messaging.

Another source of revenue? Stadium naming rights. The home to LAFC and ACFC is now called BMO Stadium. The new deal secures $10 million per year.

While we questioned the use of NFL venues (New England), the stadiums can be viable for soccer in the USA.

The Seattle Sounders FC average 34,000 fans at Lumen Field, an NFL venue. The game-day experience and atmosphere get high marks for soccer and football.

Mercedes-Benz Stadium (71,000 capacity) was built for the Atlanta Falcons and Atlanta United FC at $1.2B. It has a retractable awning designed to close in the lower bowl for soccer. The initial plan was for the soccer team to have a reduced capacity of 42,500. The Five Stripes, however, led MLS with 44,500 fans per game in 2022 (they averaged 49,000 in 2019). There's no need to close off any sections with attendance like that.

And then there's the story of the Portland Timbers and its home: Providence Park. The initial stadium was completed in 1926, primarily as an American football venue. The site has undergone three renovations since 2001. Owner Merritt Paulson invested $120 million in improvements to Providence Park. A 2019 expansion raised the capacity to 25,218 and added a multi-level facade to the East End.

The Portland Timbers have sold out every match at Providence Park since moving to MLS in 2011. The Portland Thorns set a single-game NWSL attendance record in August 2019 with a sell-out crowd of the same capacity.

In 2023, St. Louis City FC opens CITYPARK Stadium for its inaugural MLS season. The 22,500-seat venue cost $457.8 million dollars to build.

If you have been to New England in the summer, you know that the Boston Red Sox's fate impacts the entire area. The Pawtucket Red Sox were born as a Double-A Eastern League team in 1970. The franchise was twice (1990, 2003) selected as the top AAA operation in minor league baseball. The PawSox led its league in total attendance three times between 2004 and 2008.

But on February 23, 2015, the team was sold. Three years later, the club announced it would move to Worcester, Mass., 42 miles away.

What Providence did immediately was a surprise: They pivoted to soccer.

After four years of research and political wrangling, Governor Dan McKee broke a deadlocked vote to rescue the controversial stadium. Groundbreaking for the $124-million Tidewater Stadium on Seekonk River was in August 2022.

And days before the Qatar World Cup, Rhode Island FC was announced to the globe. Perhaps Rhode Island was in the team's name since the state will aid stadium construction with $60 million. Ocean State native and former USMNT player Michael Parkhurst heads the RIFC ownership group.

The stadium will have 10,500 seats for a proposed future USL Championship franchise. Financial projections assume a 7,600 average attendance. RIFC will take to the pitch in 2024.

The retrofitting for old stadiums occurs on the lower levels of soccer, too. If you watch minor league soccer on ESPN+ or elsewhere, you will see many soccer teams playing on pitches built for baseball.

The Las Vegas Lights play their home matches at Cashman Field, a stadium in downtown Las Vegas. The park was primarily used for the Las Vegas 51s, a minor league baseball team, from 1983 until 2018. It has 9,334 permanent seats and additional standing room capacity. The team has a 15-year lease agreement (expires in 2032) with the city government to use Cashman Field. The Lights began renovating the locker rooms and stadium offices before the 2019 season, with further plans to make it a soccer-specific venue.

The Tampa Bay Rowdies of the Championship play at Lang Field, a former baseball diamond. In the USL C, four teams share their stadiums with minor league baseball teams. They are Memphis 901 FC, FC Tulsa, the El Paso Locomotive FC, and New Mexico United. The latest artificial turf technology makes this crossover seamless.

The Rio Grande Valley Toros play in HEB Park. Their soccer-specific stadium is part of an entertainment complex in the off-the-beaten-track city of Edinburg, Texas. The Toros averaged 4,000 fans in its 9,700-seat stadium in 2022.

In USL League One, Union Omaha shared a stadium with a minor league baseball club in 2022. The club is looking for government help in building a 10,000-seat stadium as part of a development planned for the north side of the city.

The USL, however, is mandating soccer-specific stadiums for the Championship and League One teams by 2026. USL housed two-thirds of its 38 pro teams (Championship and League One) in soccer-specific venues in 2022. The multi-billion dollar commitment to stadiums will aid in helping build structures for the other 11 members.

USLC clubs also play in American football stadiums—with distinctive gridiron markings that fútbol lovers find unattractive. FC Tulsa, Memphis 901, the Birmingham Legion, and the Oakland Roots are four teams playing in such facilities.

Memphis 901 FC and owner Tim Howard—a former USMNT and Premier League goalkeeper—announced plans for a 10,000-seat soccer-specific stadium at Liberty Park. The Roots are also worth a mention. In addition to seeking a new venue, the team does an exceptional job on social media and in the community. Their motto is to "harness the magic of Oakland and the power of sports as a force for social good."

The Roots, the Oakland Soul women's club, and their Project 510 youth development program are jointly looking for stadium options. They will continue at Laney College until new possibilities come to fruition.

Could Oakland's last-ditch effort to retain the MLB Athletics organization be aided by housing soccer teams for its massive waterfront project?

New Mexico United—the USLC attendance leaders—had its $50-million bond issue for its downtown pitch rejected. Peter Trevisani, the team's owner, is looking at three potential stadium sites outside of downtown Albuquerque. The new deal is privately financed and will need less public help.

USL Championship attendance is mostly between 3,000 and 10,000 fans per contest. In League One (Division 3), the crowds are usually between 1,000 to 3,000 spectators.

The battle of markets and stadia also occurs in Divisions 2 and 3. In 2022, the Orange County Soccer Club (USL C) and the California United Strikers (NISA) used the soccer facilities at Irvine's Great Park.

There must be something special about the park's Championship Stadium (2,500 seats and expandable to 5K). In August 2022, the LA Galaxy made plans to secure the site for its "Los Dos" reserve team of MLS NEXT Pro. A rumored proposal would oust the other two sides and make LA Galaxy II the only professional team allowed to play at Championship Stadium.

MLS organizations are seeking optimal venues and expanding their brand footprint for MLSNP. No doubt the Galaxy was impressed with the stadium's size—and perhaps more importantly—the ability to broadcast a positive image of the team in its new streaming agreement with Apple TV.

Current tenants OCSC and Cal United and its supporters objected to the move. But criticism also came from an unlikely source: Galaxy fans. We can take that as a good sign. Soccer fans aren't tone-deaf and want the game to grow at lower levels. The Galaxy, known as MLS's most successful franchise, was unaware of this fact.

In a "rare one for the little guys," the Irvine City Council voted unanimously to allow OCSC—which averaged more than 4,000 fans in 2022—to use Championship Stadium in 2023. The Galaxy will use their same field—the track stadium—which is part of the Dignity Health Park complex in Carson, Calif.

# 26.

# Women's Soccer Pyramid

E ngland is known as the birthplace of modern soccer. They've been playing since 1859 and now boast 40,000 teams. And the country should be lauded for its promotion of global football.

For men, that is.

Women's football in England was popular in the early 20th century. Female participation, however, was later banned by the men's Football Association for "medical concerns." Not surprisingly, women's involvement declined. It took until the 1990s for the number of female players and spectators to increase.

And that's thanks to women's soccer in the United States of America, not England.

In the United States, however, there's a huge gap between pre-professional (fourth division) and Division One/NWSL.

USL has a plan to close that difference. The league announced a "comprehensive women's soccer pathway." They are launching a new second-division league—the Super League—and will expand its

Academy League for a clear path for opportunities within the USL purview.

Additionally, NISA announced plans for a Division Two League: The Women's Independent Soccer League.

The USL SL and the WISL are both slated to begin play in 2024.

The USL had 74 youth girl's teams participate in the 2021 USL Academy Cup. The new USL Academy League will feature up to six girls' divisions in 2023 and expects to increase to 12 divisions by 2026.

# 27.

# National Women's Soccer League (Division 1)

The National Women's Soccer League (NWSL) is a better investment than Major League Soccer.

Don't believe me? Ask Ron Burkle, the billionaire Southern Californian who made money in the food and grocery business.

Burkle is part owner of the NHL's Pittsburgh Penguins. He committed to be the majority owner of Sacramento Republic FC's bid to move up to MLS from the USLC. In 2019 he backed out, blaming the pandemic.

Burkle then pivoted and purchased an NWSL expansion franchise in San Diego—the Wave—which began play in 2022. MLS is more expensive and a higher risk proposition compared to the NWSL. For Burkle, an established sports owner, to opt for the fledgling women's soccer league is certainly a feather in the NWSL cap.

The Wave entered the NWSL with fellow Southern California debutante Angel City FC. Both excelled at the gate and on the field.

The Wave stayed near the top of the table in their inaugural year. Angel City had several sellouts at the 22,000-seat BMO Stadium (also home to LAFC).

Angel City boasts the largest majority female ownership group in professional sports. Their high-profile group includes Christina Aguilera, Mia Hamm, Eva Longoria, Natalie Portman and Serena Williams.

ACFC averaged 19,105 fans per game. That would've been 15th of 28 MLS teams in 2022. The Portland Thorns and its 15,545 fans? It beats three MLS clubs.

In its first match at its new home—Snapdragon Stadium on the west campus of San Diego State University—the Wave bested its LA rival, 1-0, before an NWSL record of 32,000 fans.

Founded in 2013, the NWSL had 12 teams in the 2022 campaign: Angel City FC; Chicago Red Stars; Houston Dash; Kanas City Current; NJ/NY Gotham FC; North Carolina Courage (Raleigh, N.C.); OL Reign (Seattle); Orlando Pride; Portland Thorns FC; Racing Louisville FC; San Diego Wave, and the Washington Spirit.

Interestingly, NWSL boasts two markets not served by MLS: Raleigh, N.C., and Louisville, Ky.

After winning the 2022 championship, the Portland Thorns became the first team to win three titles. North Carolina and Kansas City have won two NWSL championships. The NC Courage have collected a league-best three NWSL supporters' shields.

As with all professional sports, women's soccer has produced failed leagues. The Women's United Soccer Association (WUSA) was founded after the iconic USA Women's National Team triumph in 1999. The league ran for three seasons—from 2001 to 2003—and dissolved. Women's Professional Soccer (WPS) began in 2009 and also lasted three seasons.

When the NWSL started in 2013, the team salary cap was $200,000. The minimum and maximum salaries were $6,000 and $30,000, respectively.

Much has changed for the better.

In 2022, the salary cap was $1.1 million. The minimum salary is $35,000, and the top league salary is $75K. And in 2020, the NWSL began using "allocation money," which was $500,000 per team in the 2022 campaign. Allocation dollars allow soccer stars to be compensated higher than the maximum salary.

Like MLS, the NWSL seems to have found its footing.

In 2020 the league entered a three-year broadcasting agreement with CBS and its affiliated Paramount+ streaming service. The deal with CBS garners $4.5M annually and ends in 2023. Additionally, NWSL airs games online via the Twitch social media platform.

The NWSL has had to weather several controversies. North Carolina Courage Head Coach Paul Riley was accused of sexual coercion by multiple former players. He was fired, and his coaching license was revoked in 2021.

On August 30, 2020, MLS and NWSL announced that Dell Loy Hansen would sell Real Salt Lake, Real Monarchs, and the Utah Royals. This followed racist and sexist comments by Hansen. The Royals moved to Kansas City, but Utah was granted an NWSL team that will start in the 2024 season.

Washington Spirit co-owner Steve Baldwin resigned in October 2021. Baldwin admitted to making "some mistakes" and that he was stepping down so he wouldn't be a distraction to the team. The Spirit was the focus of concern due to its "toxic and hostile" workplace culture. Coach Richie Burke was sacked following allegations of verbal abuse.

And in October 2022, a report commissioned by NWSL was released. The Yates Report covered some of the issues mentioned above and then some. The report lambasted the league and the USSF for creating and enabling an environment where the abuse of players was "systemic."

While the report was commissioned for NWSL use, the investigation noted similar abusive behavior is also found in American youth soccer. Please read this important document here: https://tinyurl.com/ynxss68u

Since the report was issued, Portland owner Merritt Paulson—charged with covering up abuse within his organization—agreed to sell the Portland Thorns. There's pressure on other owners, league, and USSF executives to suffer consequences.

The findings in the Yates Report are troubling. The charges follow similar abuse cases of coaches and medical professionals in other women's sports, including gymnastics and swimming. Soccer can improve a toxic environment if it addresses the disturbing findings in the report.

The Yates Report has suggested an action plan to:

-Require teams to disclose misconduct to NWSL and USSF to prevent abusive coaches from joining other teams

-Eliminate non-disclosure and non-disparagement agreements that shield information about abusive coaches

-Require meaningful vetting of coaches and use the USSF's licensing authority to hold wrongdoers accountable

And in early 2023, NWSL took action on previous bad actors. The league imposed lifetime bans on four coaches: Riley, Burke, Christy Holly, and Rory Dames. And the USSF decided to implement the recommendations in the Yates Report.

2022 NWSL Playoffs and Championship: The San Diego Wave set the playoff attendance record of 26,215 in its 2-1 quarterfinal win over Chicago. The great crowds continued.

The visiting Kansas City Current upset OL Reign in the semifinals, 2-0, before 21,491 in Seattle. In Portland, the Thorns dispatched San Diego, 2-1, in front of 22,035. The home team got a late goal from Crystal Dunn—just 165 days after she gave birth—for the match-winner. The quarterfinal match in Houston—where the Dash lost to the Current, was 21,284—the fourth-best postseason crowd.

Audi Field in Washington D.C. hosted the championship match, pitting the Thorns vs. the Current. The attendance record couldn't be touched since Audi Field seats only 20,000.

Kansas City, which looked to go from worst (in 2021) to first, was overmatched the entire game. Portland prevailed, 2-0. The Thorns led in shots (18-9), corner kicks, and ball possession (53-47).

Sophia Smith tallied in the fourth minute. An own-goal was credited to KC for the match's final goal in the 56th minute.

The championship was the NWSL-best third for Portland, which made its fourth championship game appearance.

# 28.

# USL Super League (Division 2)

T he USL Super League is a professional women's soccer league that will align with the international women's soccer calendar and kick off in August 2024. The Super League aims to be the USA's first Division 2 women's soccer league.

Its unique calendar will offer soccer consumption in America's soccer "off-season." To combat the freezing temperatures across much of the country, the league will have a mid-season winter break and culminate with a June championship match.

The USL SL will provide new opportunities in women's professional soccer for players, fans, coaches, referees, staff, and executives. The league will also bring pro women's soccer to millions of fans who currently do not have it in their local communities.

In 2021, the USL hired Amanda Vandervort to lead the venture. The USL Super League will sit on top of the women's youth-to-pro pathway. The pathway includes the Super Y League, the USL Academy, and the pre-professional USL W League, which kicked off in 2022.

The USL SL plans to have 12 teams competing in its inaugural season.

# 29.

# Women's Independent Soccer League (WISL)

⌇

I n November 2022, The National Independent Soccer Association announced a future women's second-division league: the Women's Independent Soccer League. The league will start in 2024. The WISL, or "Whistle" will use the independent model to offer a new place for women's pro soccer athletes.

The WISL will be led by a longtime soccer executive: Lynn Berling-Manuel. She previously worked for Soccer America magazine, the American Youth Soccer Organization (AYSO), and the United Soccer Coaches.

There's certainly a demand for women's second-division teams and leagues. More than 1,000 colleges sponsor women's soccer. In the past, it was NWSL or bust for many prospective professionals. The new league could offer much-needed opportunities and help fill out the women's soccer pyramid in the USA.

Is the WISL too ambitious for NISA? The men's third-division league has struggled for viability. While there may be complementary symmetry between NISA and WISL, NISA's independent-driven business model has yet to prove successful.

# 30.

# Women's Premier Soccer League (Division 4)

In 2022, there were more than 220 teams competing in three leagues at the women's fourth division level. If you add the men's Division 4 squads (450), nearly 700 teams competed at the pre-professional level in 2022.

Like the men's game, Division 4 leagues aren't officially sanctioned by USSF.

The Women's Premier Soccer League (WPSL) is an amateur women's soccer league operating in the United States and Canada. The league is the world's largest women's soccer league, with 135 active teams. The WPSL is the longest-running active women's soccer league, as the 2023 season will be its 25th year.

The WPSL started as the Western Division of the old W-League before breaking away to form its own league in 1998. The WPSL consists of collegiate and post-collegiate players who currently or have played across all divisions of the NCAA, NAIA, and NJCAA.

WPSL alumnae include Shannon Box, Brandi Chastain, Julie Foudy, Kristine Lilly, and Heather Mitts.

League President Sean Jones estimated that teams spend from as little as $15,000 up to 100K to field a WPSL team. In an interview with The Athletic, he noted team expenditures didn't necessarily match success on and off the field.

In February 2023, the league announced WPSL PRO, a new third division circuit. The league expects to start in 2025 with 10 teams.

2022 WPSL Championship: The California Storm defeated the Colorado Rapids Women in the WPSL Championship Final, 3-1, on July 24, 2022, at Neal Patterson Stadium on the campus of Oklahoma State University.

The championship was the Storm's fourth crown since joining as a founding league member in 1998, but its first since 2004. The Davis, Calif.-based club has won the most WPSL history titles.

Alexandra Klos opened the scoring in the 14th minute for the Storm. The score remained 1-0 at the break.

Shiloh Miller tied the match in the 48th minute for the Rapids. Yet Brenda Uribe netted the eventual game-winner three minutes later. The Storm's Misty Ramirez added an insurance tally in the 78th minute for the championship match's final goal.

Sixteen teams advanced to the WPSL playoffs. The Rapids advanced to the WPSL Championship Final after topping the South Jersey Elite Barons FC, 2-0. In the other semifinal match, the Storm edged the Nashville Rhythm F.C, 1-0.

The Storm were later named the WPSL franchise of the year. The team's regular season record was an unbeaten 8-0-2. The club tallied 29 goals and allowed just seven scores from its opponents. The Storm also sold more than 4,000 tickets to their home games, the profits of which fund the next year's community and autism-friendly soccer clinics.

# 31.

# United Women's Soccer (Division 4)

~~~

United Women's Soccer (UWS) is a national pro-am league composed of clubs within the United States and Canada. According to its website, the UWS boasts high-level competition for college players, aspiring and former professionals, and international stars.

UWS fielded 49 teams competing in six conferences. Its amateur League 2 has 47 clubs and serves as a feeder to the pre-professional UWS.

Could UWS or another Division 4 league move up the pyramid? According to league executive director Stephanie Cleaves a change is not imminent, partly due to economics.

"It takes $40,000 to probably $100,000 to operate a team at this level," Cleaves said in an interview with The Athletic. "And then at the D-III level that we're exploring and it's like $800,000 to $1.2 million."

The league can claim to be the first to have a player go directly from the fourth division to the top pick in NWSL Santa Clarita (Calif.) Blue Heat's Alyssa Thompson went #1 overall to Angel City FC.

2022 UWS Championship: With a 2-1 victory over the Calgary Foothills at Lusitano Stadium in Metuchen, N.J., the Chicago Mustangs capped off an undefeated season with a UWS National Championship.

The achievement came in the club's second season in UWS. The defeat was Calgary's first of the year.

Calgary scored first in the 36th minute after Saoria Miller poked in a pass from Jayden Berg. Just before halftime, however, Nina Nicosia assisted tournament MVP Julia Simon for the equalizer.

The championship-deciding goal came in the 50th minute. Substitute Ainsley Ahmadian floated a shot from the right wing to the left corner of the net for the match-winner.

# 32.

# USL W League (Division 4)

T he USL W League is a pre-professional league similar to the USL 2 league on the men's side. In its inaugural 2022 season, the W League featured 44 teams playing in seven conferences.

Two of the strongest organizations advanced to the first USL W Championship game. South Georgia Tormenta FC had just one loss in the regular season. The organization is bullish on minor league soccer. The Tormenta also sponsors men's teams in the USL League One and League 2.

But the star of the inaugural season of the W League: the Minnesota Aurora. They played their home games at the Minnesota Viking's practice facility, averaged more than 5,000 fans per home match, and had the biggest crowd ever at TCO Stadium for the league finale.

The Aurora won the Heartland Division and boasted an undefeated season until the final match. Minnesota values communications, evidenced by an updated roster, a solid website, and full game stories following each match. They also exude professionalism in the presentation of their team/business.

124

There was buzz that Minnesota was in consideration for a 2024 NWSL expansion franchise. While the Aurora didn't make the final cut, don't be surprised if the organization graduates to a higher level at some point.

Seven players that competed in the 2022 USL W League season were picked in the 2023 NWSL Draft. Of the 43 W League alums registered for the four-round draft, two were selected in the first round, one in the second, three in the third and one in the fourth.

Nineteen expansion sides will join the W League for the 2023 season. Clubs, cities, and stadiums see the value of sponsoring women's pre-professional squads, often in tandem with a USL men's squad.

2022 USL W League Championship: The inaugural 2022 USL W League Final was won by the South Georgia Tormenta FC after its 2-1 win over host Minnesota Aurora FC on July 23, 2022. The match was played before a record 6,489 fans at TCO Stadium in Eagan, Minn.

South Georgia closed the year with an 8-1-4 record and handed the home club its first defeat of the year. Minnesota Aurora ended its season with an 11-1-1 mark.

Jaida Nyby had a brace for Tormenta. She scored in the second overtime for the game-winner. Nyby netted the match's first score off an assist from teammate Lauren O'Hearn.

For Minnesota, Mackenzie Langdok assisted Addison Symonds for their goal. The Aurora outshot the visitors, 20-7.

Tormenta FC defeated the home-standing Greenville (S.C.) Liberty SC, 4-1, in a semifinal match. In the other semifinal, Minnesota Aurora FC edged McLean Soccer (Va.) 1-0.

There was nothing minor about the launch of the Minnesota Aurora FC. The team captivated its fans and did not lose until its final game. Pictured above is Kristelle Yewah versus South Georgia Tormenta FC in the inaugural USL W League title match. (Photograph courtesy of Minnesota Aurora.)

# 33.

# The Soccer Federations

The International Federation of Association Football, or FIFA, governs global soccer. The organization runs the World Cups, age group championships, and Olympic competitions. FIFA also oversees leagues throughout the world.

The organization was founded in 1904 and is based in Switzerland, like the International Olympic Committee. There are 211 FIFA member nations and six regional subsidiaries: Asia and Australia (AFC): Africa (CAF); South America (CONMEBOL); Oceania (OFC); Europe (UEFA), and North America (CONCACAF).

CONCACAF stands for the confederation of North, Central American, and Caribbean Association Football. The association is based in Miami and serves 41 member nations.

Mexico and the United States have dominated the region on the men's side. The United States, not surprisingly, is the flagship program for women in CONCACAF. Canada is now strong on both the male and female sides, too. The Canadian men's team qualified for the 2022 World Cup, their first since 1986.

One could argue that FIFA has hindered the development of the women's game. FIFA executives have disparaged the women's game in public. There still is no Women's Club World Cup. FIFA has allowed artificial turf for its women's World Cup, but not for the men. The pay inequity between the men's and women's World Cups is substantial.

Corruption seems synonymous with sporting federations, and FIFA and CONCACAF are no exception. The conspicuous awarding of the 2022 World Cup to Qatar—a tiny but wealthy Arab nation with little sporting history or infrastructure—is a prime example of a dubious bidding practice. On the same day in 2010, FIFA awarded the 2018 World Cup to Russia.

Thanks to the United States Justice Department, some of FIFA's corruption has been exposed. Several FIFA representatives were implicated in taking bribes in exchange for voting for Russia getting the 2018 men's World Cup. Many FIFA members were bounced from the organization. Some served prison time.

CONCACAF was at the root of the problem, too. Former federation President Jack Warner from Trinidad and Tobago solicited bribes and skimmed profits. Warner schemed to use the voting power of CONCACAF and its 41 nations for individual financial gains rather than developing soccer.

When Warner went too far, his deputy—American Chuck Blazer—turned him in. Blazer was involved in the same illegal schemes and died before he was sentenced in 2017. The USA has been unsuccessful in extraditing Warner from the Caribbean.

There was more troubling news just weeks before the 2022 Qatar World Cup. Reports by the AP and Reuters noted that Qataris were paying for fans to attend the World Cup to provide good PR for the host nation. The "fan leaders"—as many as 50 from each nation— were asked to post good things about Qatar and the World Cup on social media. They were also asked to report negative posts to Qatari authorities.

After word leaked out about the scheme? Qatar reneged on paying the promised per-diems to the fan leaders.

Swiss news source SRF then delivered a blockbuster that hundreds of millions of dollars were spent by Qatar to spy on FIFA officials. Their concern was to prevent the country from losing the games after the bribery scandal emerged.

Homosexuality is illegal in Qatar. Reports stated that 6,500 immigrants have died in stadium and infrastructure construction in preparing the nation for hosting the "Mundial." The country was criticized for migrant working conditions. Foreigners make up 90 percent of the Qatari workforce. The nation's "kefala" system has been compared to both indentured servitude and slavery.

There are few nations that can bid alone for World Cups and Olympics in the 21st century. It costs billions of dollars to fund such extravagant competitions. Other than the USA and a few Western nations, Russia and China seem to be on the shortlist for most bidding cycles.

Russia has made a mockery of fair play. They were caught creating and operating a system that allowed their athletes to cheat by passing doping tests at their 2014 Sochi Winter Games. Cheating can give the perception of national superiority.

The phenomenon of using sports to hide the faults of a country is often called "sports washing."

The most famous sports washer was Adolph Hitler. He used Germany hosting the 1936 Olympics as a propaganda tool. Hitler promoted his Nazi Party with great fanfare and claimed the superiority of his Aryan nation.

His theory was flawed, however. African American Jesse Owens won four track and field gold medals and was the star of Hitler's Olympic games.

Sports washing is alleged to have occurred in global soccer, too. A Netflix series linked the 1978 World Cup in Argentina—where FIFA cooperated with a dictatorship—and Qatar to the practice.

"Sports washing is a big issue now," said journalist David Conn in "FIFA Uncovered," a documentary series released in 2022. "When you look back at the 1978 World Cup, the 1936 Olympics, and now Qatar, I think it becomes more disturbing."

Conn later lumped Russia 2018 as part of the sports washing allegation. Russia and Qatar were awarded their Cups in 2010 ahead of England and the USA—which produced superior bids.

The combined nations' bid is becoming a popular alternative for large sports events. Australia and New Zealand, for example, will share hosting duties for the 2023 Women's World Cup. In 2026, the USA, Mexico, and Canada will host the Men's World Cup. This trend makes great financial and logistical sense to share both the burden of hosting the World Cup and the benefits host nations reap from it.

The Qatar example, on a positive note, exemplifies FIFA's mission of spreading soccer around the globe. Yes, the costs and proceeds of the World Cup are exorbitant.

UEFA — with its regional club and national team tournaments — takes in more money than FIFA. It's likely one reason FIFA proposed a World Cup every two years, rather than the current four.

And with business/sports/politics in mind, a brief look at the European Super League is in order.

The top European clubs proposed a tournament without the necessary qualification requirements of the current UEFA Champions League. The proposal was made in 2021 when teams were hurting financially due to Covid.

Every business likes a sure thing. The 12 "founding owners" wanted automatic tournament entry to guarantee the huge television dollars. The Super League would quash the traditional competition and hierarchal aspects evident in global football.

And the league did not get off the ground. The English teams, partly due to fan backlash, backed out first. Three clubs still support the concept: Barcelona, Juventus and Real Madrid.

The website Superleague.com is still active. And oddly, all of the teams that backed out are still featured. UEFA may have won this battle, but perhaps not the Super League war. For more on the Super

League, see the Apple TV four-part series "Super League: War for Football."

# 34.

# United States Men's National Team

⌇

A mericans cherish the 1980 USA gold medal hockey team or the famous 1992 men's basketball dream team. But in soccer, the national teams are followed passionately in *every* Olympics and World Cup.

Soccer is unique because there is an intense passion for the international game over clubs. The USA is no different. There are two "America's Teams" in the country: the USMNT and the USWNT.

The United States men's national soccer team (USMNT) represents the U.S. in men's international soccer competitions.

The American men have appeared in 11 FIFA World Cups—including the first in 1930—when they reached the semifinals. The USMNT returned in 1934 and 1950, defeating England 1–0 in the latter, but did not qualify again until 1990. The 40-year gap was broken in 1989 after Paul Caligiuri's "shot heard round the world" in Trinidad.

As the tournament host in 1994, the U.S. received an automatic berth. The Yanks advanced to the knockout stage before losing to Brazil in the round of 16. The American men qualified for seven consecutive appearances from 1990 to 2014—an achievement shared with only seven other nations.

The Stars and Stripes reached the quarterfinals in 2002 and controversially lost to Germany. In the 2009 Confederations Cup—a "test run" before South Africa hosted the World Cup the following year—the USMNT eliminated top-ranked Spain in the semifinals before losing to Brazil in the final. This was the USMNT's only appearance in the final of a major intercontinental tournament.

The 2018 team failed to qualify for the 2018 World Cup hosted by Russia. Under the direction of Coach Gregg Berhalter, fielding a young and talented squad, the Yanks qualified for the 2022 Qatar World Cup and reached the knockout round.

The USA has won seven CONCACAF Gold Cups—the Federation's signature tournament. The USMNT captured the inaugural edition of the CONCACAF Nations League (2021) and finished fourth in two Copa Américas (1995 and 2016). The Copa América is South America's championship, but teams from outside the continent are often invited.

In Olympic men's soccer, unlike the women, the competition features under-23-year-old athletes and three overage players. The Americans missed the previous three Olympics (2012, 2016, 2020) but have qualified for the 2024 games in Paris.

How do you fix the USMNT? If you still think it needs fixing, "What Happened to the USMNT" has a few answers. The book by authors Steven G. Mandis and Sarah Parsons Wolter suggests getting the top Americans in the "top 5" global soccer leagues: Premier League, UK;

La Liga, Italy; Serie A, Spain; Bundesliga, Germany, and Ligue 1, France.

The good news is more Americans are playing in the top five. This trend increased from eight in 2014 to 12 in 2022.

The authors also note that familiarity with moving players from one club (Bayern Munich as an example) to the national team (Germany) is paramount. Unlike the Bundesliga and Germany, however, the Americans will likely never have more than a handful of players from the same club. Bringing two defenders who play together on a club, for example, onto a national team builds positive player/team chemistry.

One factor not covered in "What Happened to the USMNT" is the familiarity the Yanks have developed being in the U.S. Youth program. Many of the 2022 team formed friendships and synchronicity with the USSF youth teams that aid the current USMNT.

Another good question: when will MLS surpass one or more of these five leagues if it hasn't already?

# Top Five Highlights in USMNT history

*According to Alexi Lalas, State of the Union Podcast, August 11, 2022*

## 5. Italy 1, USA 0 1990

Scrappy young yanks, debutantes on the global stage, hang with the host and eventual winners.

## 4. USA 1, England 0, 1950

The Americans were huge underdogs, but USA's Joe Gaetjens tallied the match's solitary goal.

## 3. USA 2, Colombia 1, 1994

Denim-clad Americans downed heavily favored Colombia at the Rose Bowl, aided by a fatal own-goal (literally and figuratively) from Andres Escobar.

## 2. USA 1, Algeria 0, 2010

Landon Donavan goes coast-to-coast and provides "pure American joy" to the nation.

## 1. USA 2, Mexico 0, 2002

"Dos a Cero" on the global stage is the most significant win over its fierce North American rivals. And this win secured the USA's best-ever showing (quarterfinals) in the modern World Cup era, too.

# 35.

# United States Women's National Team

The U.S. women's national soccer team (USWNT) represents the USA in international women's soccer. The United States Soccer Federation governs the team, and they compete in CONCACAF and FIFA.

The USMNT has a respectable history. The American men, however, usually are measured against the incredibly successful U.S. women.

The USWNT is *the* most successful program in international soccer. The American women have won Women's World Cup titles (1991, 1999, 2015, and 2019), four Olympic gold medals (1996, 2004, 2008, and 2012), and nine CONCACAF Gold Cups.

The Yanks medaled in every World Cup and Olympic tournament in women's soccer from 1991 to 2015 before being knocked out in the quarterfinal of the 2016 Summer Olympics.

The USWNT was the U.S. Olympic Committee's Team of the Year in 1997 and 1999. Sports Illustrated chose the entire team as 1999 Sportswomen of the Year for its usual Sportsman of the Year honor.

In addition to Title IX, the University of North Carolina was a massive asset to the success of the USWNT. Managed by Anson Dorrance, the Tar Heels were the dominant NCAA women's soccer program as the USWNT succeeded in the 1990s and beyond.

UNC was the preeminent destination for the country's best women's soccer talent. Dorrance also coached the USWNT to the 1991 World Cup championship and brought many of his current and former athletes to the national team. This trend continued as the USWNT often fielded a core of Tar Heels.

Of the 39 players in the 2022 USWNT pool, only two had no affiliation with NWSL clubs. Lindsey Horan and Catarina Macario play for Super Club Lyon in the French first-division league.

Women's soccer is improving around the globe. Super clubs like Lyon, Barcelona, Real Madrid, Chelsea, and Arsenal are now recognized as the best clubs in the world. Such programs are acclaimed for their superior talent identification and training infrastructure.

The Americans had an advantage with Title IX and the US collegiate system as a feeder to the USWNT. No longer. The NWSL, the USSF, and other leagues will need to invest in youth development to compete with the rest of the world.

In February 2022, numerous current and former members of the USWNT, including Megan Rapinoe and Alex Morgan, settled a pay-inequity lawsuit with the U.S. Soccer Federation for $24 million. Male and female national team players will be paid equally moving forward.

This new agreement paid immediate dividends. The USMNT and the USWNT shared at least $6.5 million each after the men advanced to the 2022 World Cup knockout round. That payday was more than the American women earned from winning the 2015 and 2019 World Cups ($6 million combined).

# PART III.

## ATTACKING/

## FINISHING

## THIRD

*Indoor, Rivalries, Media, Glossary of*
*Terms, and the Future*

# 36.

# Indoor Soccer in the USA

~~~

Indoor soccer has a rich history in North America. The game, also dubbed arena soccer, was a natural for American arenas that housed hockey teams. The indoor game used the dasher boards from hockey, put down artificial turf, added two soccer goals, and voila!

The dasher boards are unique to mini football and can create a "pinball machine" dynamic on a soccer pitch, usually 200x85 feet.

Field soccer features 11 players, but it's reduced to between five and seven players a side indoors. Arena soccer is overseen by the Confederation of MiniFootball (CPM). There are international competitions, but FIFA does not recognize the USA arena variation.

FIFA recognizes futsal, an indoor game born in Uruguay in 1930. The game is similar to regular soccer in that there are touchlines like soccer and corner kicks. Futsal also features kick-ins instead of throw-ins. A futsal match can be played on a basketball court with no dasher boards.

While there is no professional futsal in the USA, the game is becoming more popular in the States in recreational leagues. Futsal is now recognized as an excellent way for players to develop skills that can translate to the field game.

Professional indoor soccer is said to have started in 1971 when the North American Soccer League organized a series of exhibition tournaments. Three years later, the first broadcast of a game between NASL players and the Soviet Red Army appeared on ABC's "Wide World of Sports."

In October 1977, Ed Tepper and Earl Foreman formed the Major Indoor Soccer League. The MISL ran from 1978 to 1992. The MISL averaged more than 7,000 fans per game, and that increased to more than 9,000 in attendance in the postseason.

Those crowds raised the eyebrows of many, including the NASL. In response, the league introduced an indoor campaign to complement its outdoor NASL season. The San Diego Sockers defeated the New York Cosmos for their third straight indoor title, having won the NASL Indoor title in 1981–82 and the MISL title in 1982–83. The 1983–84 NASL indoor season was the fourth and last in league history.

The Sockers then joined the MISL after the NASL died. They continued their success with eight more championships. Only one franchise lasted the entirety of MISL: the Baltimore Blast, which played its first two seasons in Houston.

As for individuals, one name stands out: Steve Zungul. He defected from Yugoslavia to the United States to ostensibly play in the NASL. A FIFA sanction for leaving his home club prevented him from joining the NASL, but had no bearing in the unregulated MISL.

Zungul made a seamless transition to indoor. From 1978 to 1990, he tallied 652 goals, dished 472 assists, and earned five Most Valuable Player awards. As such, he earned the nickname the "Lord of All Indoors." Zungul was a 2023 inductee to the National Soccer Hall of Fame.

# 37.

# Major Arena Soccer League and Other Leagues

T here are many leagues that tried to reinvent the magic of MISL. The acronyms are too many to list here. Since 2008, the Major Arena Soccer League has been the preeminent first-division men's indoor league. The MASL season runs from November to April.

The MASL features 14 teams in three divisions: West, Central, and East. The San Diego Sockers and Baltimore Blast join nostalgic indoor names such as the Dallas Sidekicks, St. Louis Ambush, Kansas City Comets, and Tacoma Stars.

The MASL features no Canadian sides but has two franchises in Mexico: Chihuahua and Monterrey. The league live streams its games on MASL TV Live, which is accessible on YouTube.

In most cases, MASL eschews the large venues currently used for NBA and NHL teams. Prior to the Covid 19 pandemic, average playoff attendance surpassed 4,000 fans. Regular season attendance hovers at 2,000 customers, so choosing the proper arena makes sense.

The 16-time indoor champion Sockers are opening a new arena in 2023. After playing primarily at the San Diego (now Penchanga) Sports Arena, the team is moving 35 miles north to the city of Oceanside. Frontwave Arena seats 7,600 people and features 16 premium luxury suites.

Josh Hughes has toiled in the MASL, USL 2 (then PDL), NPSL, USL Championship, USL League One, and the defunct NASL 2.0. Hughes played collegiately at NCAA Division III Berry College. A defender, he earned all-conference and CoSIDA Academic All-America recognition as a senior.

Hughes may not have the stats of Steve Zungul, but he also made a successful transition from field soccer to indoors. He notes that playing for the Baltimore Blast as the highlight of his professional soccer career.

"Indoor soccer was an entirely different beast to play," Hughes said. "I've seen and met many professional outdoor players who couldn't translate their games to indoor because of the steep learning curve. There is a lot more structure in the way indoor is played and understanding all the different rules is a daunting task."

Most salaries can range from $15,000 to $55,000. USMNT legend Landon Donovan was paid $250K when he joined the Sockers in 2019. Donovan has since stayed in the city. First as the coach and now as an executive with the San Diego Loyal of the USL Championship.

MASL also offers lower-level leagues dubbed MASL 2 and 3—their denoted levels of the indoor pyramid.

Premier Arena Soccer League (PASL) operates on the Division 3 level. The PASL fielded 17 men's teams and 15 women's clubs in 2022. Most of the clubs are in Texas and the Midwest United States.

The National Indoor Soccer League launched in 2021. NISL, with all teams based in the Southeast USA, has seven men's and six women's teams slated for play in the 2023 season.

The Western Indoor Soccer League entered its eighth year in 2022-23 with seven men's clubs operating in Oregon and Washington.

2022 MASL Championship: The San Diego Sockers won their second straight Major Arena Soccer League title after a 4-3 victory over the Florida Tropics in front of a crowd of 3,105 at Penchanga Arena on May 8, 2022.

"It's a great feeling," said team captain Kraig Chiles, who scored the game-winning goal at 6:19 of the third quarter. The San Diego native had a team-leading eight goals in the playoffs and earned Finals MVP honors.

"I'm so proud of every player on this team," said owner and head coach Phil Salvagio, who won his sixth championship, "We battled all year long with a target on our backs. And in the end, we have back-to-back Ron Newman Cups."

The Sockers celebrated back-to-back championships for the first time in their MASL tenure. The title was their sixth since restarting in 2009. San Diego went 23-0-1 in the regular season, winning the MASL Shield as the top team in the regular season.

# 38.

# The Soccer Rivalries

T he name "Clásico" derives from the Spanish Clásico soccer rivalry between Barcelona and Real Madrid, dubbed "El Clásico." In Argentina, River Plate and Boca Juniors form the heralded Superclásico derby.

In MLS, the California Clásico is the name given to the rivalry between the LA Galaxy and the San Jose Earthquakes. The LA vs. Bay Area battle was heated from 2001 to 2005 when the two clubs combined for four league championships. Heading to 2023, the Galaxy leads the series with 45 wins to 32 defeats. There have been 18 draws. For San Jose's game in September 2022, Stanford Stadium and 44,200 fans played host to the derby.

With the addition of LAFC in 2018, El Tráfico has taken over as the preeminent rival to the Galaxy. This derby name comes from the infamous automobile traffic congestion that plagues the City of the Angels. It replaced the SuperClásico after Chivas USA disbanded.

The Galaxy will go back to the future when it plays LAFC at its old home stadium—the Rose Bowl—to open the 2023 campaign. It's expected the match will attract an MLS record of 90,000 fans.

On the East Coast, the Hudson River Derby pits the Red Bulls vs. NYCFC. With three teams now in Texas and two in Florida, MLS is ripe for more derbys and the passion that comes with them.

The most unique men's rivalry, however, involves *three* teams in the Pacific Northwest—also known as Cascadia. The Cascadia Cup is the name of the trophy created in 2004 by the supporters of the Portland Timbers, Seattle Sounders, and Vancouver Whitecaps.

As mentioned earlier, the three clubs share a history from the 1970s in the NASL. The Sounders have won seven Cascadia Cups, which dates to the teams competing in the USL.

And don't sleep on the derby between just Seattle and Portland clubs —on both the men's and women's sides. OL Reign and the Portland Thorns have built a well-attended and passionate derby in NWSL. The Timbers and Sounders? Yes, that's a rivalry, too.

The expansion teams of 2022 from Southern California—Angel City FC and the San Diego Wave—might have already established their battle as the NWSL's foremost rivalry. Sold-out games in Los Angeles and the biggest crowd in league history in San Diego (32,000) have set the table for a fantastic derby.

# 39.

# Nothing beats the USA vs. Mexico

I buried the lead. The greatest rivalry in North American soccer features the men's national teams from the USA and Mexico.

The Yanks and El Tri first competed in 1934. The teams have met 74 times. Mexico leads the overall series 36–22–16. The U.S., however, has held the edge since 2000 with a 17–9–7 mark.

The CONCACAF Gold Cup was started in 1991 to crown a regional champion. Since then, Mexico has won eight titles to seven for the Americans.

Even before MLS started, USA-Mexico was a box office success. Aided by El Tri fans, 90,000 spectators regularly ventured to see the teams compete in the Rose Bowl, for example. And the games translated to eyeballs for English and Spanish-speaking television viewers.

Soccer competes for popularity in the USA, but it's easily numero uno south of the border. The El Tri national team is a 24/7/365 business covered feverishly by the Mexican media.

True rivalries ebb and flow. El Tri dominated the battles for the 40-year span (1950-90) when the Americans didn't qualify for the World Cup. Since then, the two countries have been the dominant forces in CONCACAF.

In more recent years, the Yanks have won trophies. The USA defeated Mexico in the final match of the CONCACAF Gold Cup and the inaugural Nations League—both contested in 2021 (due to delays from Covid 19).

The USA dealt another blow to Mexico when the Seattle Sounders FC captured the CONCACAF Champions League. The Sounders defeated visiting Pumas of Liga MX, 3-0, on May 5, 2022. That win secured the Sounders a spot in the FIFA Club World Cup, the first American side to qualify for the prestigious event.

The tournament brings together the top clubs in the region and has been dominated by teams from Liga MX. Mexican sides had won the first 13 titles since the CONCACAF Champions League began in 2008.

Get ready for more USA-Mexico competition. MLS and Liga MX will expand the Leagues Cup in 2023 to include all 47 clubs. The tournament will take one month to complete as each league shuts down late in the summer.

The new format gives a bye to the Liga MX and MLS champions into the knockout round. The other 45 clubs will be drawn into 15 three-team pods. MLS teams will host, and Supporters' Shield standings will seed the teams before advancing to the knockout round.

The Championship match is scheduled for August 19. The champion, runner-up, and third-place finisher will qualify for the CONCACAF Champions League.

A television series about the USA-Mexico men's soccer rivalry was released during the 2022 World Cup. "Good Rivals" is a three-part series that covers what some call the greatest international sports competition. It's available on Prime Video.

There are valid concerns about the rivalry moving forward. With both nations qualifying for the 2026 World Cup, there will be no "home-and-home" qualifiers this term. Additionally, as the World Cup grows, more CONCACAF teams will qualify for the games. It's a numbers game, and changing dynamics puts the future of competitive USA vs. Mexico home-and-home qualifying matches in danger.

Nevertheless, we are worrying about 2029 and beyond. In the meantime, enjoy the friendlies, Nation's League, and Gold Cups matches between El Tri and the Stars and Stripes.

# 40.

# The USA Women and Rivals

I t's been hard for the dominant American women to find a long-time foe. To be a rival, each competing team needs to win now and then.

In the early days, the USA's stiffest competition came from North Korea (what happened to them?), China and Norway. Sweden has probably been the team's most consistent competitor. Brazil was a powerhouse for a minute. And now European teams like England, Spain, France, and Germany are fielding outstanding sides.

More than 86.000 fans watched the USA women—the reigning World Cup champions—and England (recently crowned UEFA champs) in October 2022 at England's national stadium: Wembley. The highly anticipated match was at the center of controversy since the Yates Report was released earlier in the week. The Brits edged the USA 2-1. The Americans had a superb match-tying goal that was overturned by as offside by video review.

The CONCACAF region is quite top-heavy. The long-dominant Americans now have a formidable foe in Canada. The Yanks have fallen to the Reds on a few occasions.

Will the El Tri vs. the Stars and Stripes women ever become a rivalry on the women's side? The Mexicans haven't advanced out of the group stage in their three World Cup appearances. Mexico did, however, finish second in the 1998 and 2010 CONCACAF Championships.

The Mexican Federation initially participated—along with USA and Canada—in launching the NWSL. The Mexicans pulled out in 2016 after starting their own league: Liga MX Femenil. The women's clubs are aligned with their Liga MX counterparts. Since the league began in 2017, UANL has earned four league championships.

In 2021, Liga MX Femenil allowed two foreign players per roster. The next year, Mia Fishel topped the Apertura tournament with 17 goals. Fellow Yank teammate Bianca Sierra also competed for UANL.

# 41.

# Media and Fútbol in America

One of the early critiques of soccer on American television? There were no timeouts or many stoppages during the 90 minutes of a game. That meant broadcasters could not leave the game to sell advertising spots in its traditional way. The rest of the sporting world, however, adapted to the game. Two revenue generators were scrolling ad insertions that didn't take the game off the screen and using on-field signage visible to viewers.

I took time, but American television adapted, too. Instead of signing a traditional media deal focused on linear television, the league announced a 10-year, $2.5B partnership with Apple TV. The paid streaming agreement begins with the 2023 season.

As part of the deal, MLS will forego local media rights. It's a forward-looking deal where MLS sees its core fans already on streaming services.

Does this mean every viewer will need to add a paid service to see any MLS games? No, the league will offer free games on Apple TV and farm out matches to cable and traditional linear/broadcast outlets, too. In fact, 40% of the league's matches will be *in front* of the Apple TV paywall. That means free to viewers, soccer fans.

Most games will be on Saturdays and Wednesdays. Some contests will be on linear television, too. The video quality will improve, and more cameras will be at each game (from 9 to 15). MLS will hire 12 broadcast crews for both English and Spanish broadcasts. With Montreal in tow, French broadcast teams will be employed, too. Perhaps with the Brazilian market in mind, MLS is looking at Portuguese crews, too. Game announcers will be on-site to cover the games.

The cost of the package is $99 per year or $14.99 per month. If you are already an Apple TV+ subscriber, the MLS package is reduced to $79 and $12.99/monthly. MLS Season ticket holders will have free access to the new service.

One caveat of the agreement is that fans can access MLS broadcasts anywhere. No more being blacked out on vacation. No more needing an IP address when you visit Paris or the Philippines. The package goes with *you*.

In December 2022, MLS announced partnerships with linear and cable carriers. Garber stated the deals were "supplemental to Apple partnership."

TSN (English) and RBS (French) in Canada will televise MLS games on their platforms. Fox Sports and TelevisaUnivision will carry Spanish-speaking broadcasts in the USA. Most of TelevisaUnivision's live coverage will be of the newly expanded Leagues Cup.

EPSN, with the MLS since 1996, will no longer broadcast the league's games. Fox Sports retained its relationship with MLS.

Remember that every MLS game can be viewed with the Apple package. However, Fox will televise the following:

-34 regular-season games annually and eight Audi MLS Cup playoff matches each season on FOX/FS1/FOX Deportes

-15 regular-season matches each year on FOX (the most ever by one English language over-the-air network in MLS history)

-MLS Cup every year on FOX and FOX Deportes

-Leagues Cup: 10 Group Stage, four Round of 32, and two Round of 16 matches each tournament on FS1

-Highlight rights, editorial coverage, and cross-marketing support.

That's a lot of MLS soccer for casual fans. And a "whip-around" show with league-wide highlights will be a new feature for viewers. Additionally, the broadcasts will be "national" in scope. The announcers will be picked by MLS rather than hiring local talent. Imagine watching a Sunday NFL TV broadcast instead of your hometown baseball telecast.

If you look at the sum MLS garnered in its deal, one could see it as pocket change compared to the NFL, NBA, or MLB.

The late Grant Wahl, however, brought up an interesting point in his Aug. 19, 2022 Substack column. American broadcasters are banking on global soccer.

"When you add up the payments for soccer rights, which are much more fragmented than other major sports, U.S. companies are now paying significantly more overall for soccer rights than they are for ice hockey rights (the NHL is getting $625 million/year from its American rights-holders). Just the list of soccer rights (MLS, Premier League, NWSL, Univision, etc.) is worth $1.44 billion annually," noted Wahl.

Yes, the $1.4B is not going directly to MLS or to Americans, for that matter. The investment should be seen as an investment in soccer. And interest in soccer translates to kids playing soccer, following a La Liga team, attending your local minor league club's game, and being a fan of the nearest MLS team.

In that same column, yours truly penned a question to the late scribe:

*You have been a stalwart of the soccer sports journalism scene. Obviously, your Substack business model signals a change in the way we consume sports content. I'm curious about what your thoughts are on the short-term and long-term outlook of the soccer media landscape?*

*-Bob Lowe*

Wahl's response:

*Well, the TV conversation at the top of this column suggests that the long-term outlook for televised soccer in the U.S. is quite good! As for soccer journalism in the U.S. and journalism in general, that's a bit murkier in the long term. Local newspapers are largely struggling. Free sites have a lot of annoying ads, clickbait, and dumb stories. The outlets that actually produce stories you're going to remember are typically subscription sites like the ones on Substack (including mine), The Athletic, and the New York Times (which are actually the same company now). As much as the sport of soccer is growing in the U.S. right now, you'd hope that U.S. soccer journalism would be growing with it. But that's sadly not the case. That's why I hope enough people will subscribe to GrantWahl.com!*

Critics claimed MLS punted to streaming because it couldn't secure a $300M deal annually in the traditional media rights model.

Consider how media consumption has changed in recent years. What will the climate be like in 2033?

And if you plan to abstain from paying for MLS on a streaming platform, get ready for more change. The USMNT and USWNT got new homes, too. The USSF secured an eight-year deal with TBS, TNT, and HBO Max. According to the Sports Business Journal, they will broadcast more than 20 games annually and will pay about $26 million annually for the privilege. Telemundo signed a four-year deal to broadcast U.S. Soccer properties in Spanish.

Protagonist Soccer, a group dedicated to minor league soccer in the USA—interviewed Wahl in 2022. He's a renowned journalist, but this interview also illustrates what a savvy business mind he had. Take a listen to this podcast: https://tinyurl.com/4jnp6zec

# 42.

# Confessions of a Sports Media Consumer

~~~

Remember my reference to watching soccer in the 1980s and 90s? It often was viewing the USMNT on Univision, a Spanish language outlet, or nothing. There was no demand for the product in English in the USA.

The sports viewing landscape has changed mightily in the past 30 years. There are certainly more soccer games—and all sporting events—available to watch than ever before.

And don't sleep on watching games in Spanish, even if you don't know the language. Goal and "goooooooooooal" are universal. Good television sports broadcasters give you the basics by simply indicating who has possession of the ball. And most of us can figure out the basics of the on-screen Chyron graphics.

And we've paid for that privilege. Let me give you an example of an average sports fanatic and his choices in using specific sports properties over the past 15 years. It happens to be the author.

We were already DirecTV subscribers with many of the sports packages. NFL Sunday Ticket was added so I could enjoy every out-of-market game for my favorite team. The $250 annual cost was easily justified since attending one game in person could be a greater expense than that price.

In about 2013, I got the MLB audio package. This was a relatively cheap option, and I got the benefit of hearing the iconic Vin Scully, just like in the days of my youth, with a transistor radio under the pillow. A few years later, we upgraded to the MLBTV video option. That's another $250. But can you beat that with a season of 162 games? What a value!

Next, the soccer storm would come in full force. Every time there is a CONCACAF event—be it World Cup qualifying or the Gold Cup—it's our continent's federation that holds rights, not the USSF.

That used to mean purchasing BeIN Sports (owned by Qatar) in your sports packages to watch away qualifying matches. In 2022, Paramount+ got the rights. So write that check for $6.95 per month. Real fans *must* see every USMNT match.

The undervalued U.S. Open Cup is compelling. I gotta see some of these Division 4 teams on the big stage! Please take my $9.95/month, ESPN+! Plus, you get the ESPN Insider written content, too. And scores of other leagues and sports. (Pickleball is on the move, folks!)

I was a reluctant English Premier League viewer. Pulisic to Chelsea will pique your interest. And Leeds getting Jesse Marsch (later sacked), Brenden Aaronson, Tyler Adams, and Weston McKennie? The dedicated fan must follow Leeds USA!

161

NBC Sports has Premiership rights in the USA. The games stream on Peacock (still holding out), and NBC's USA Network shows games since they scuttled the NBC Sports Network in 2022.

And in this time of subscription services, have you ever taken a trip to a foreign land? If so, you know our USA subscriptions are invalid in Canada, Barbados, England, or the Turks and Caicos.

But there is a hack: VPN! Yes, you'll need to pay another $10 a month to fool folks that you are still in the USA. It seems as though that media companies are catching onto this solution, too, as they are implementing smarter firewalls.

Sports media junkies need to be passionate about managing their subscriptions and the changing menu of options. The media landscape changes daily.

Sometimes, the sports media gods hand you a solid. A game or tournament gets bought by Apple TV or Amazon Prime? Phew, you might already have that subscription. Additionally, suppose you are a Sirius XM subscriber. In that case, you might not have purchased it for soccer, but channel 157 has Jason Davis and his "United States of Soccer" and other fútbol content.

For many, the MLS and Apple agreement will be welcomed, simply for the chance to watch anywhere on Earth.

Let's move over to the written word. Some still subscribe to the local newspaper and Sports Illustrated. Both are shells of their glory days. Perhaps you subscribe to the online editions of the Los Angeles Times and the New York Times. Many avid sports pay a fee to The Athletic, which employs some of the best sports journalists, to get detailed coverage of their teams. Cha-ching!

Have you heard of Substack? Journalists charge a monthly fee for written content. I currently pay for two sports subscriptions on Substack. Need some freebies? Most sports podcasts are free for now.

Isn't it all exhausting? A soccer fan may burn more stress calories than a player after 90 minutes of action!

For those who hoped cord-cutting would be cheaper than your cable or satellite bill? So sorry, folks.

And when the MLS Season Pass was available on Apple TV? The author immediately plopped down the $79.99 for the privilege.

Other than MLS, here's a look at where you can find which league in the USA:

Bein Sports: African Cup of Nations, Turkish League, France's Ligue 1.

ABC/ESPN/ESPN+: Bundesliga, U.S. Open Cup, Emirates FA Cup, La Liga, UFSL Championship, USL League One, Indian Super League, La Liga, FA Cup, EFL, Eredvise, A League Men and Women, NCAA Men's and Women's Soccer.

HBO Max, TBS/TNT: USWMNT and USMNT Friendlies, She Believes Cup.

NBC/USA Network/Peacock: English Premier League, USWMNT and USMNT Friendlies, She Believes Cup in Spanish (Peacock).

Paramount Plus/CBSSN/CBS: UEFA Champions League, Europa League, Europa Conference League, Serie A, NWSL (also on Twitch).

Telemundo (Spanish): English Premier League, USWMNT and USMNT Friendlies, She Believes Cup.

Univision (Spanish): Champions League, Liga MX, Liga MX Femenil.

# 43.

# Do you Wanna Own at Team in the UK?

*"I've only been an owner of a football club for a very short time. So I've found it to be time-consuming, emotionally exhausting, financially idiotic, and utterly addictive."*

*-Ryan Reynolds, co-owner of Wrexham AFC*

Forget about "Ted Lasso." That's fiction, folks. You can watch the real deal with "Welcome to Wrexham."

There are many American owners of foreign soccer teams. But Ryan Reynolds and Rob McElhenney didn't buy themselves a Premier League team or an American franchise.

The pair purchased Welsh side Wrexham AFC for £2 million ($2.4M USA). Founded in 1964, Wrexham is the Welsh club. The tea8 seeks promotion after spending the past 15 years in the National League— the fifth tier of the English football league system.

You can read some details here and watch their documentary, produced by Reynolds and McElhenney, "Welcome to Wrexham."

The series is on FX and streaming on Hulu. Watch the preview/trailer here: https://tinyurl.com/248dv4u6

Reynolds and McElhenney are essentially no different than Dan Hoedeman of Minneapolis SC, or Dennis Crowley of the Kingston Stockade. They had no experience running a soccer team and would've failed author Malcolm Gladwell's 10,000-hour test.

Yet they all are similar in that they all have a passion for adventure, sports, and the journey. It's fascinating to watch Wrexham's progress.

Not surprisingly, Wrexham now has an avid fan base in the USA. ESPN started covering the team's games, including competition in the FA Cup, the UK's version of the U.S. Open Cup.

On an early Saturday morning stateside, Wrexham battled Blyth, who play one level below the National League. Blyth's Crofts Park, nestled in a Northumberland town, reminds viewers of Keyworth Stadium of Detroit City FC, or any early-round U.S. Open Cup match. Additionally, anyone who has toiled in college sports communication could relate to the temporary scaffolding needed to accommodate the ESPN crew.

Before 2,787 fans on Oct. 15, 2022, the teams tied, 1-1. The home-standing Spartans had the better of possession and scoring chances. Yet a deflected free kick from 25 yards out by Tom O'Connor put the visitors ahead in the 76th minute.

In the 89th minute, Blyth converted a corner kick to the far corner for the equalizer. Unlike the U.S. Open Cup, no penalty kicks decide who advances. Instead, a "replay" was slated for three days later at Wrexham's Racecourse Grounds. And Wrexham, after building an early 3-0 advantage on goals from newfound TV stars Paul Mullin and Ollie Palmer, had to hold on for a 3-2 victory. The attendance was 6,845 (246 traveling from Blyth) for the match.

Wrexham continued in the FA Cup. The team defeated Coventry City of the second division Championship and advanced further than any other club from the National League.

Not Surprisingly, Wrexham announced that the club will tour the United States in the summer of 2023. The trip makes sense as the television series has expanded its popularity stateside. And the matches vs. MLS teams should make for compelling future episodes of the series.

Reynolds and McElhenney are (so far) beloved in Wrexham. If the team climbs the pyramid, they will be heroes.

By contrast, American foreign owners like John Henry (Liverpool), the Glazers (Manchester United) and Stan Kroenke (Arsenal) are despised. Why? Supporters claim these Yankees took their beloved community club from them only for money.

The Premier League, which Reynolds says is the goal for Wrexham, has become a league of moderate spenders versus the billionaire SuperClubs at the top. Be careful what you wish for, fellas.

# 44.

# An Ode to the American Soccer Player

*"Don't give up on your dreams, or your dreams will give up on you."*

—*John Wooden*

Hats off to the American soccer players who have reached the precipice, Christian Pulisic and Alex Morgan, for example. Our brightest stars rightfully deserve the acclaim and compensation they earn.

The best of sport, however, is the athlete chasing the dream without a large contract. Perhaps one of the best examples of striving for excellence and perseverance is the story of Jay DeMerit.

DeMerit played college soccer for the University of Illinois at Chicago. But, after not being drafted by Major League Soccer, he went abroad to reach his athletic dreams. DeMerit took the advice of a European teammate and decided to use his EU work status (due to a Danish grandfather). With $1,800 in his pocket, he went to England in 2003 to find a soccer club.

The defender began playing in the ninth tier of English soccer for Southall. He earned only about $60 per week to start. In July 2004,

DeMerit joined Northwood, a seventh-tier side, for their pre-season games. During one match, DeMerit impressed then-Watford manager Ray Lewington enough to earn a two-week trial.

DeMerit proceeded to play 211 games for Watford over six seasons. He helped the club win the 2007 Championship Playoff Final before 65,000 fans to secure promotion to the Premier League. After his release from Watford, he was the first player signed by the Vancouver Whitecaps FC for their entrance into MLS. DeMerit played four seasons before retiring after a 10-year pro career.

The defender earned 25 caps for the USMNT from 2007 to 2011. DeMerit was part of squads that won the 2007 CONCACAF Gold Cup and were second at the 2009 FIFA Confederations Cup. He also played on USA teams in the 2007 Copa América and the 2010 FIFA World Cup.

DeMerit's story was so good it became Hollywood-worthy. "Rise and Shine: The Jay Demerit Story" was released to favorable reviews in 2011. You can watch it here:

https://www.youtube.com/watch?v=GtSYAUn2I7I

For every Jay DeMerit, however, hundreds of other men and women are hoping for a similar ascent. Josh Hughes, for example, had an analogous rise within the American ranks—falling just short of MLS.

Being an aspiring soccer professional is a full-time job. For those unaware, soccer is one of the rare male sports where height and weight aren't embellished. The reason? A player needs incredible fitness to play 90 minutes of soccer at a high level. A man to be listed at 5-9 and 145 pounds is not a bad thing.

169

The average American minor league player needs a side hustle to pay the bills. Many pro teams offer free housing to team members, which is a huge benefit. Additionally, players can make extra money doing promotional appearances for the team in the community.

In most cases, however, players make extra funds within the game of soccer. Being connected to the soccer community, a player can coach a youth team in his area. And many squads are directly linked to such youth programs. A savvy minor leaguer will earn coaching licensures during his/her playing career, which can pay dividends in the future.

A drawback to coaching while pursuing a player career? A pro soccer player needs to conserve energy for training and games. Being on your feet at youth team practices or games doesn't help a player perform at 100 percent in a pro soccer match.

It's safe to say that a tiny percentage of current minor leaguers are working in traditional careers. For example, you can find a few mortgage brokers or real estate agents on rosters. It takes dedication to earn a living at one, much less two, jobs.

Which begs the question: What about family life?

A common theme is a spouse or partner foregoing a normal life for their significant other. It's certainly a sacrifice to put trial contracts or $15K salaries ahead of traditional middle-class life of reliable income, home mortgages, medical benefits, and a retirement plan.

Hughes is still single. Yet he has picked up soccer coaching certificates if he chooses that path later. He is an Academic All-American, has a chemistry degree, and recently started computer programming. He will be fine.

But hats off to the many athletes chasing pro athletic dreams in their 20s. How many of us can say we played professional sports? There are your 30s to your 60s to stash your nest egg.

And USL announcing a player's agreement with both the Championship and League One is a great step for current and future players. Here's hoping other leagues sign onto these agreements.

After having a standout career as an NCAA Division III soccer player at Berry (Ga.) College, Josh Hughes has toiled in the minor leagues of American soccer. Shown above playing for the storied Baltimore Blast of MASL, Hughes previously played in the USL PDL (now USL 2), NPSL, the second rendition of NASL, USL One, and the USL Championship. (Photo courtesy of the Baltimore Blast.)

# Top Rated "Soccer Cities" in the USA

**Greensboro, N.C.** – The Gate City is a destination for youth soccer tournaments and collegiate championships. A women's and men's fourth division teams call the Gate City home.

**Frisco, Texas** – Greater Dallas city hosts the U.S. Soccer Hall of Fame and FC Dallas, the preeminent incubator of elite male soccer talent in the USA.

**Atlanta, Ga**. – Atlanta United averages 45,000 fans and captured an MLS Cup in year two. Case closed.

**Chattanooga, Tenn**. – Two men's third division teams reached the semifinals in 2022; documented excellent attendance and other minor league and college soccer teams in town.

**Chicago, Ill.** – When you house the United States Soccer Federation, an NWSL and MLS team? You can't be ignored.

**Washington, D.C.** – The storied history of DC United, Audi Field, and the Washington Spirit catapult the nation's capital to our register.

**Seattle, Wash**. – Lumen Field may be an NFL venue, but the Sounders and OL Reign bring wins, fans, and atmosphere.

**Portland, Ore.** – The Rose City boasts championship NWSL and MLS teams and ardent fan support at iconic Providence Park. Bonus points for the University of Portland women's program.

**Kansas City, Mo**. – MLS and NWSL championship teams play in separate soccer-specific venues. KC had the best national TV ratings for the 2022 World Cup.

**Los Angeles** – The LA Galaxy now has market competition with two exciting tenants at BMO Stadium. The Rose Bowl, Coliseum, UCLA, World Cup, and Olympic games aid its rich soccer history.

**Statesboro, Ga.** – South Georgia Tormenta won a USL League One and USL W League title in 2022. The city of 33,500 is also home to NCAA Division 1 men's and women's teams at Georgia Southern University. Statesboro is hereby dubbed the best "pound-for-pound" soccer city in the USA.

*Honorable mention/keep an eye on Charlotte, Columbus, Oakland and Miami, and New York City.*

# 45.

# A Look to the Future

T here are many reasons that the State of Soccer is strong, fellow Americans.

**Player Development**

On the women's side, the NWSL still primarily drafts and employs athletes who played for NCAA soccer programs. In essence, the league is where the MLS was in the 1990s as far as collegians filling out the rosters.

But that is changing.

Olivia Moultrie took a different path in joining the Portland Thorns. The prodigy turned professional at age 13. She became the youngest player to score a goal in NWSL when she tallied against the Houston Dash at age 16.

Angel City FC traded for the 2023 first-overall pick in the player draft. They selected Alyssa Thompson from nearby Harvard-Westlake High School.

Matching the men's game, expect the youth development programs to produce more athletes who choose to go pro instead of pursuing a collegiate career. Additionally, well-financed foreign clubs will look to the USA to enhance their programs.

Before the Covid pandemic, more than two dozen American women played pro soccer in Europe. A handful of the biggest stars were slated to play in the UK's Women's Super League. Only three Americans played in the WSL in 2022. That number will rise in the post-pandemic world.

The two proposed second-division leagues—the WISL and the USL Super League—will bridge the gap in the women's pyramid. A third division WPSL PRO, and youth academies' continuing their growth, will also aid development.

Perhaps there will soon be a U.S. Open Cup, or something similar, on the women's side. The women's game could use such a tournament, just like we need a FIFA Women's World Cup.

Women's leagues and teams will add more academies or similar development throughout the nation. This change is terrific for players and families. In the past, top-level talent often had to spend more time traveling to an academy than playing and practicing. And remember that these are kids.

There are still under-the-radar soccer athletes rising to the top in the USA. Goalkeeper Matt Turner didn't get serious about soccer until he was 16. He didn't crack the lineup at Fairfield University until he was an upperclassman. Turner went undrafted in the SuperDraft.

LAFC center-back Aaron Long was a late bloomer who played at unheralded UC Riverside. Before blossoming with the Red Bulls, he struggled in his early pro years and worked construction in the USL offseason.

Eight members of the 2022 USMT played collegiate soccer in the USA. (Three players did both academy and college.) That's a significant change from the 100 percent collegiate on the 1990 World Cup team.

"The American development programs are better and better," said Sebastian Dremmler, a long-time Bayern Munich youth coach in 2018. "We will see the final result in five to 10 years. In 2026 the USA will have a powerful national team."

A handful of clubs have shown little or no interest in the most recent MLS SuperDrafts. LAFC is one example. Perhaps that will change when they implement their MLSNP squad.

If you need a specific example of the potential of American collegians, look no further than Jack Elliott of the Philadelphia Union. The 6-6 defender scored two goals in the 2022 MLS Cup. Elliott was picked in the fourth round of the 2017 SuperDraft. Two franchises passed on selecting any player before Elliot was chosen.

Everyone comes from somewhere in soccer. Jay DeMerit and Jack Elliott prove that point.

An episode on the Protagonist Soccer podcast shortly after the 2022 World Cup focused on NISA player development. The discussion praised the efforts of Chattanooga FC's youth program and suggested a potential opportunity for the fledgling league.

The great thing about soccer is that there are opportunities worldwide. Remember that developing and transferring players isn't limited to selling them to MLS or the Premier League. The host suggested forming relationships in Africa and Asia as an alternative.

Television revenue is minimal in the third division. Player transfer fees could help NISA and their teams' bottom lines, in addition to ticket sales, merchandise, and sponsorships.

-Postscript to Level 4 Soccer

All soccer clubs are businesses. Each business places different priorities in certain areas. Some clubs strive to break even or make a profit.

Fans, however, can get frustrated with the lack of finding basic game and league information.

This is not a knock on anyone or the league. I get that most of the soccer community's passion is simply to get players on the field competing. Opportunities for player development and promotion are paramount for many clubs.

However, the lack of accessible contact information—and the apparent understaffing of communications professionals to post updated news, game stories, player bio information, schedules, etc.— is a void.

There's some sentiment in Division 4 that these teams and leagues deserve official sanctioning by the United States Soccer Federation.

There are standards for teams to compete in certain leagues or levels. Guidelines for field dimensions and pitch quality, minimum financial requirements for owners, and player safety standards requiring athletic training professionals are examples that teams are expected to meet.

My unsolicited professional advice? Implement a set of *minimum communications requirements* for teams and leagues at Division 4.

Teams are not doing as well as they should be in meeting traditional sports information gathering. All clubs should have posted a roster with player headshots and basic biographies of each athlete, including hometown, college, etc., of each athlete. Schedules and results should be updated promptly. If there is no live stats or game tracker software for matches, a box score should be posted ASAP.

Posting a game report and statistics on a web page is essential. The entry should include general match information, score by-halves, goal-scoring information, shots, saves including individual credit to goalkeepers, corner kicks, cautions, team records after the match, and attendance.

A team representative should also report game results to traditional media as well. Most notably, local television stations and newspapers. Yes, there are reports of the newspaper industry's decline. They likely don't have the staff to cover games live, but including coverage of local minor league teams is a value-added benefit to their readers. And content in the sports section of the paper is free advertising.

Some U 23 clubs affiliated with year-round soccer programs look at Division 4 as a "loss leader." The fourth division team is branded with the established youth club. For them, having a top-quality U 23 team—chock full of athletes from the area's top universities—is a great carrot to motivate the younger age groups. If a club is focused on its "day job" of year-round soccer programs, it makes sense to use this approach.

This model may be acceptable, but not doing the team, fans, league, players, or communities a favor by not striving to do better. Is it not better to play in front of enthusiastic crowds instead of "friends and family?"

**Ancillary Soccer**

In October 2022, USMNT legend Clint Dempsey and NBA star Chris Paul announced a new 7-on-7 summer soccer tournament with a grand prize of $1 million. The event debuts in June of 2023 and will be called "The Soccer Tournament."

If you are familiar with the TBT hoops tournament, it's similar to that. The same company will run the event to be held at WakeMed Soccer Park in Cary, N.C. The four-day tournament will field teams in group play and then, like the World Cup, advance to a knockout round.

Is this a game-changer? Absolutely not. It does, however, demonstrate the marketability of soccer improving in the USA.

In January 2023, Wrexham AFC announced they would include an entry in the 32-team tournament.

## International Soccer

Just days away from the Qatar World Cup, former FIFA Commissioner Sepp Blatter made headlines. Adding fuel to the fire, Blatter said it was a mistake to award the Cup to the tiny nation.

Was it a mea culpa for human rights? A stand against corruption or the criminality that brought the games to Qatar in the first place?

Of course not.

Blatter indicated that Qatar was too "small" to put on the games. That didn't cross his mind a decade ago when they won the bid? Blatter said this after all the expensive stadiums had been constructed and the country had paid billions for infrastructure.

Ironically, the former FIFA commissioner criticized the best aspect of the 2022 games: the small footprint. Fans and teams were just minutes away from all venues. There were hundreds of thousands of soccer fanatics in such a small area. An optimist would view this as one of the few positives. It was a unique soccer oasis that may never be replicated.

Then again, one wonders why folks should listen to a man banned from FIFA until 2028.

And Qatar and its flaws were cannon fodder for critics.

Pete Pattison of The Guardian has reported extensively on the societal concerns in Qatar. He noted that recently changed laws have improved the lot for immigrant workers. On the ground, however, change has been slower.

Human rights, racism, worker's rights, democracy, and equality are top of mind during World Cups. Russia and China come to mind, too, on this subject. Despite their shortcomings, they've been awarded and hosted many high-profile events.

However, Western nations have recently taken a step toward authoritarianism and away from human rights. The term "glass houses" comes to mind as every nation should strive for progress on these fronts.

Officials connected to both the 1996 Atlanta and 2002 Salt Lake City Olympics were caught in bribery scandals. FIFA corruption included an American: Chuck Blazer.

Perhaps CONCACAF has begun righting its ship. Many past bribes were paid under the lie that payments go to aid soccer in the bribed nations. The federation debuted its Nations League in 2021. The promotion-relegation tournament allows more games and exposure for its 41 nations. Kudos to CONCACAF for helping the smaller nations of its membership.

Nevertheless, soccer consistently promotes initiatives combatting racism and championing human rights. FIFA, national federations, corporate sponsors, fans, and athletes can use their powerful platforms to keep demanding better. This trend needs to continue with consequences for bad actors/nations.

Here's hoping FIFA never repeats its blunder in choosing a nation like Qatar for a future World Cup. Aside from the bribery charges and other controversies with the Gulf nation, there's the exorbitant cost associated with the 2022 tournament. World Cups usually don't make a profit. Qatar, however, spent a reported $300 billion for the games with a benefit of $7.5 billion.

In January 2023, the New York Times reported that Fox Sports might have used inside information and bribery to secure the broadcast rights to the World Cup. If true, is anyone surprised?

Curious minds want to know if Fox also agreed to report favorably of Qatar. Their coverage of soccer *games* was acceptable. Their lack of criticism of FIFA or the host nation during the tournament was journalistic malpractice. Was that a quid-pro-quo?

History indicates that money trumps human rights and sensibility every time with FIFA. The lone nation as host, is likely still a reality. FIFA President Gianni Infantino gushed about the success of the Qatar World Cup. What will he do to top it: Saudi Arabia in 2030? Would anyone be surprised if FIFA tabbed the crown kings of sports washing for that World Cup?

"Sports allows itself to be essentially bought by regimes with human rights issues, rather than using its power to take a stance against that," said David Conn in "FIFA Uncovered."

## NWSL and USWNT

It's officially NWSL 2.0 time. West Coast expansion, improved distribution of games, and impressive attendance are reasons for optimism.

International soccer teams—especially the U.S. women's national team—have led global women's soccer. It's now time, however, for club soccer to pick up the slack, which means NWSL stateside. The league is—top to bottom—easily the best collection of teams in the world.

The 2022 NWSL Championship match was the most watched broadcast in league history. In a coveted primetime spot (8 p.m. EST) on CBS, the telecast averaged 915,000 viewers, a 71-percent increase from 2021. These impressive numbers came with popular college football available to television viewers at the same time.

The 2023 season is the last of NWSL's $4.5 million deal with CBS. With MLS's deal with Apple TV—and the increasing value of sports properties—expect the new deal to be exponentially higher.

According to the NWSL, 30 investor groups showed interest in seeking an expansion franchise. In January 2023, the league granted three expansion cities: Boston, San Francisco, and Utah. The Boston and the San Francisco Bay Area groups agreed to pay a record $50 million franchise fee.

The Utah and Bay Area teams will join the league in 2024, with Boston joining at a later time. Utah ownership is expected to pay between $2 million and $5 million, an arrangement related to losing its team to Kansas City.

Fifty million dollars for an NWSL franchise is an impressive and substantial fee. But others believe the numbers will continue to escalate.

"As far as I'm concerned, we are going to be the first women's franchise with a valuation of $1 billion," said Angel City FC President and co-founder Julie Uhrman. "There's no better investment today than women's sports."

While that is a lofty goal for Angel City, it isn't impossible. LAFC, which shares BMO Stadium with ACFC, was valued at #1 billion by Forbes.

Angel City has secured $40 million in sponsorships. They renewed 90% of its season tickets from year one. ACFC's unique business model donates 10% of revenue back into their community.

The USWNT will head to New Zealand and Australia for the 2023 Women's World Cup. The Stars and Stripes seek to be the first nation (men or women) to win three straight World Cups. The Americans will face formidable competition, however.

While the soccer world waits for the first FIFA Women's Soccer Club World Cup, there was good news in the Western Hemisphere. In early 2023, CONCACAF announced that its 2024 W Gold Cup will include four guest teams from CONMEBOL/South America for the 12-team tournament.

## MLS and the USMNT

The last word on pro-rel? We have our version here in the USA. The biggest cities have the richest owners and best stadiums and play in the first division. The market dictates the terms for the second and third division teams and leagues. Teams will continue to move up and down the pyramid.

Meanwhile, MLS has advanced to 3.0 mode. The new Apple TV contract, the changes in the Leagues Cup, a potential World Cup-style group format for playoffs, improving quality of play, and adding MLS NEXT Pro are reasons for great optimism.

In 2022, leaguewide attendance topped 10 million fans for the first time.

The future proposal of round-robin proposal for MLS playoffs is intriguing. Soccer will always have different tweaks in the USA. Tinkering with the postseason could be a worthy endeavor since the sports-watching crowd gets diverted to other offerings in October.

The soccer-specific stadium commitment has been a boon to the league. And MLS now has "champagne problems" as many venues aren't big enough for some regular season games.

The Beckham signing was crucial to creating interest in the MLS 2.0 era. The quality of MLS play has improved dramatically since then. Will global stars like Messi and Cristiano Ronaldo come to America for their fútbol curtain call? International stars will need to perform if they come to the USA.

If the global superstar(s) arrive, and if more rivalries heat up, expect NFL and other venues to host more future games. Has MLS Cup outgrown many of the current league venues?

You could make the case that European football is better, but MLS is a safer business bet.

How many Apple TV subscriptions will be sold if Messi—clad in Inter Miami pink—comes to MLS? The numbers—and revenue—could be jaw-dropping.

NASL needed Pele in 1975. MLS needed Beckham in 2007. Which stars come to America now? It's simply a bonus.

The USMNT had a decent showing at the 2022 World Cup. Oddsmakers predicted that the young Americans would not reach the knockout round. They did.

In the round of 16, the Netherlands exposed the USA's youth and deficiencies in handing the team a 3-1 defeat.

During the World Cup, public reporting indicated Gio Reyna was unhappy with a reserve role. We then found out his parents (some might say helicopter parents) meddled in the situation. Berhalter also added fuel to the fire when he returned to the USA.

Let's go through the timeline of this USMNT soap opera:

-Berhalter advises Gio Reyna that he won't be starting and he will have a reserve role for the 2022 World Cup.

-Gio loafs during training sessions and exhibits a poor attitude.

-Soccer dad/USMNT legend/Austin FC executive Claudio Reyna then sends a barrage of texts to many—including current USMNT Sporting Director Earnie Stewart and General Manager Brian McBride—complaining about his son's lack of playing time.

-Berhalter directs Gio to apologize to his team. He does, but his teammates find it hollow.

-Berhalter inexplicably mentions the incident at a leadership conference stateside after the USA is eliminated from the World Cup.

-Soccer mom/former USWNT player Danielle Reyna informs Stewart about an incident regarding Berhlater kicking his then-girlfriend 30 years ago. Danielle claims she brought this up to illustrate that her son wasn't as bad as Berhalter at a young age.

-Stewart opens an investigation into Berhalter's abuse incident.

-Stewart takes a job in his native Netherlands and the USSF does not retain general manager McBride.

-Claudio Reyna is demoted at Austin FC.

-The selection of a new sporting director and permanent USMNT coach is put in limbo. The USMNT will be without a permanent coach until the summer of 2023.

Meanwhile, the Yanks appear poised for a great showing in 2026 when the world comes to North America for the World Cup. The USMNT possesses a formidable core foundation at goalkeeper, the midfield, and on the wings.

Certain members of the 2022 squad will be the following ages in four years: Brenden Aaronson, 25; Tyler Adams, 27; Cameron Carter-Vickers, 28; Sergino Dest, 25; Weston McKennie; 27; Yunus Musah, 23; Christian Pulisic, 27; Gio Reyna; 23; Antonee Robinson, 28; Joe Scally, 23; and Tim Weah, 26.

The World Cup is a "young man's game." U.S. Soccer's youth development has a talented and deep player pool. The stars from 2022 will likely be pushed—and perhaps replaced—by teenagers during the Qatar World Cup.

The USSF should also send its best possible lineup to the 2024 Olympics in Paris. On paper, the Yanks have an under-23 roster that is medal-worthy. Aaronson, Reyna, Scally, Musah, and Dest are some athletes who might be available for the Olympics. Club teams, however, aren't required to release players for the Olympic games.

In January 2023, CONCACAF and CONMEBOL announced two agreements that will aid men's soccer in the Western hemisphere, affecting both national teams and clubs.

The 2024 Copa América will include six nations from CONCACAF with 10 South American sides. The six teams will be the top finishers in the 2023-24 CONCACAF Nation's League.

The USMNT was seeking better competition in preparation for the 2026 World Cup. Being in the Copa América is the perfect antidote and may help attract a top-tier coach for the team. The USA is expected to host either most or all of the tournament.

The two federations will also launch a four-team club championship in 2024. Two teams from each federation will compete in the tournament. The clubs will qualify through existing CONMEBOL and CONCACAF competitions.

Money and television drive these announcements. The Copa América competition, however, will be a needed bridge between redundant regional tournaments and the World Cup for the USMNT. Additionally, the club competition will require MLS to improve its product on a bigger stage.

Do Americans like soccer? The most tickets purchased for the 2022 Qatar World Cup by a foreign nation were from the United States. The above photograph of American fans was taken before the USA-England match, which yielded more than 20 million viewers stateside. (Photo by Ben Alkaly.)

# 46.

# A Novices Guide to Soccer Nomenclature

**Ball-watching** – This is when a player is focused on the flight of the ball rather than the player he/she is supposed to mark.

**Balon d'or and balon d'or feminine** – The annual awards, presented by a French magazine, denoting the world's best male and female soccer players, respectively.

**Bicycle kick** – This occurs when an offensive player, with his/her back to the goal, leaves the ground and fires above the waist in an acrobatic shot attempt. In Spanish: bicicleta.

**Booked** – This happens when a referee holds up a yellow or red card to a player.

**Brace** – A soccer player records a "brace" after being credited with two goals in a game.

**Break** – Occurs when a team quickly advances toward the opponent's goal before the defense has a chance to set itself.

191

**Cap** – A term used in soccer to indicate a player suiting up for his/her national team. For example: "Yunus Musah earned his 50th cap today."

**Capo** – Is short for a "captain" who leads cheering in a supporter's section for a team.

**Chip** – A term use when a lofted shot is attempted over the goalkeeper.

**Clean sheet** – When a team allows no goals to the opposition—a shutout.

**Cross** – This is a pass by a player to a teammate near the front of the goal area.

**Corner kick** – After a ball last touched by the defensive and goes out of bounds on its end line—taken by a team in its offensive end at one of two corner areas.

**Derby** – Pronounced "dar-bee" in Brit-speak is a match between two teams from the same city or region. Often called a classic or clásico.

**Direct free kicks** – These follow a foul by the defense and can be played directly on goal.

**Counter** – This is an attack after the defensive team regains possession.

**False 9** – Occurs when a squad deploys a player at a deeper position than the traditional spot of a striker, or number nine.

**Formation** – Indicates how the players set up from defense to offense and not including the goalkeeper (A 4-4-2, for example, indicates four defenders, four midfielders, and two forwards.).

**Foul** – This is a violation that results in a free kick for the other team.

Goal kick – This occurs when the goalkeeper boots the ball from within the 18-yard box after the offense caused the ball to go over the end line.

**Hat trick** – A soccer player nets three goals in a game.

**Header** – When a player uses his forehead to direct the ball as a shot or pass.

**Indirect free kick** – Occurs after a violation (offsides) and the ball must be touched by one other player than the kicker in order to score.

**Inswinger** – Is a corner kick or cross taken to curve toward the goal.

**Mark** – A posture taken by a defensive player in order to prevent the opponent from getting a better advantage for his/her team.

**Mixer** – After a corner or free kick taken, there's often pinball zaniness in front of the goal called the mixer.

**Nine** – The jersey number 9 is often used by the traditional striker/forward.

**Nutmeg** – Is a clever move by a player to pass the ball through the opponent's legs and keep possession of the ball on the other side.

**Offsides** – Occurs when a player in an offensive player doesn't have two opponents between him/her and the goal when the ball is passed to said player. Typically, the goalkeeper plus one defender indicates an offside position, but it can be any two players if the keeper is out of position.

**Olympic foal or olimpico** – Is a goal scored directly off of a free or corner kick that doesn't touch any other player before.

**Outswinger** – A cross or corner kick taken to curve away from the goal.

**Park the bus, bunker, or pack it in** – Are defensive tactics where a less-talented club positions its players in the defensive third to thwart the offense.

**Penalty shot** – Happens because of a foul by the defense committed within his/her penalty area.

**Penalty kicks** – Usually is used only in a tournament that require a team needing to advance. Five players from each team shoot and more if tied thereafter.

**Playing out of the back** – Is a philosophy where a side makes numerous passes in its defensive end in order to gradually enter its offensive zone.

**Play on or play advantage** – A referee spots a foul but allows the offensive player who kept possession to continue a scoring chance.

**Red card** – Awarded to a player after a serious foul. Usually, an egregious or aggressive foul, or a foul negating a clear goal-scoring opportunity. A second yellow card in a game results in a red card, too. In addition to being ejected from the game, a red-carded player must miss his/her next contest, too.

**Result** – Any positive outcome, either a win (three points) or a draw (one point) for a team in a game.

**Tackling** – Simply taking the ball from the opponent.

**Ten** – The number 10 is often worn by a playmaking forward or midfielder.

**Third** – The soccer field is unofficially divided in the three zones, with the offensive third being the attacking zone.

**Throw-in** – Is a restart where a player throws the ball behind his/her head with two hands. It happens after the opposing team caused the ball to out of bounds on the sideline.

**Touch line** – A boundary line commonly referred to as "sidelines" in other American sports.

**Unlucky** – Often shouted by a coach with a faux British accent after one of his/her players does something solid on the pitch, but it does result in a goal or even a completed pass.

**VAR** – Video Assistant Referee technology which allows calls to be verified or corrected by a video officiating crew.

**Volley** – A ball kicked by player while it's in the air.

**Wingers** – The outside forwards who are often responsible for crossing the ball to teammates in front of the goal.

**Worldie** – Is a goal of incredible quality. Spanish-speakers often say "golazo."

**Yellow card** – A caution card booking to a player who commits a dangerous or unsporting play.

# 47.

# 2022 Qatar World Cup Addendum

T he 2022 World Cup group stage was both competitive and entertaining. No team won all three matches for the first time in the 32-team format. The biggest upset occurred on day two when Saudi Arabia beat eventual champion Argentina, 2-0

The Americans were undefeated in Group B. The Yanks settled for a 1-1 tie vs. Wales. The much-anticipated match vs. England ended in a scoreless draw. The USMNT needed a win over Iran to advance to the knockout round. Pulisic scored in the 38th minute, and the Stars and Stripes held off a late Iranian push for the 1-0 victory.

The USMNT drew the Netherlands in the round of 16. The Americans played formidable defense in the group stage but not against Holland. The Dutch capitalized on three defensive blunders for its three goals. Pulisic assisted Haji Wright to cut the margin to 2-1 in the 76th minute. Denzel Dumfries tallied five minutes later for the final 3-1 result.

As play reached the quarterfinals, five European teams, two South American and one African nation, Morocco, remained.

As Argentina progressed, the groundswell of support for Lionel Messi and Co. grew.

While Argentina was ousting the Dutch on PKs, a surreal tragedy occurred in the press area. Grant Wahl suffered an aortic aneurysm and could not be revived. Known for his journalism excellence and selfless care for others, Wahl was mourned by all.

"To Grant soccer was more than just a sport," said Dr. Celine Gounder—Wahl's wife—on CBS. "It was a way of understanding people and where they were coming from. I want people to remember him as a kind, generous person who was really dedicated to social justice."

In the other quarterfinal matches, Croatia stunned Brazil on penalty kicks. France edged rival England, 2-1. And Morocco stunned Portugal, 1-0.

Julian Alvarez scored twice to lead Argentina to a 3-0 victory over Croatia. But it was Messi who stole the show with a goal and an incredible assist on the final goal. He collected the ball near midfield and was closely marked by Alexis MacAlister. Messi toyed with the defender as he dribbled for 50-yards before placing a pass in front of the six-yard box for Alvarez to get his second tally,

On the next day, France ended Morocco's Cinderella run with a 2-0 win. In the 79th minute, Randal Kolo Muani sealed the victory for Le Bleu with the other goal. Theo Hernandez opened the scoring in the fifth minute.

The final match between Argentina and the French pitted the two best teams in the tournament. Additionally, the individual battle between Messi and Kylian Mbappe added intrigue. Frenchman Mbappe is known as the best young player in the world. Messi, perhaps the greatest footballer of all time, sought his first World Cup title.

Argentina dominated play in the first half and built up a 2-0 advantage. Mbappe, who recorded a hat trick, converted a penalty kick in the 80th minute. Ninety seconds later, he tied the match.

The game went to extra time. Messi knocked home a rebound to put Argentina ahead in the 100th minute. Mbappe nailed his second penalty 10 minutes later. Both teams had chances in the waning minutes.

Messi and Argentina won the penalty kick shootout, 4-2.

The match was one of the most viewed in American history. An average of 51.56 million watched the game. Those combined numbers reveal viewers on Fox (25.8M), Spanish language Telemundo (16.78M) and streaming (9M)

And Messi's fantastic play raised a question: Is he the best-ever soccer player?

After Pelé died ten days later, the question resurfaced.

Pelé led Brazil to three World Cups titles to Messi's one. The Brazilian tallied 709 career goals to the Argentinian's 695.

Pelé's soccer career and influence is unsurpassed. Period.

Sport—and the Beautiful Game—can bring out the best in humanity. The United States isn't known as a soccer nation, but it has helped develop the women's game in pay quality and equity. And without the U.S. Justice Department? FIFIA and its regional federations would be stealing more. Some justice beats none.

And the United States will continue to play a larger role in global soccer. American influence—of business savvy and service to sport—will also help the $tate of Soccer on the planet.

It takes a village. Athletes, coaches, administrators and fans need to influence that future.

Who helped quash the Super League? British football supporters who love their club, community and traditions. And it was the fans that brought the Philadelphia Union to MLS. LA Galaxy supporters voiced displeasure when a minor league team was going to get booted out of its stadium.

People have the power!

Let's end with a favorite American Outlaws chant regularly heard at U.S. national team matches: "We Love Ya." Watch and sing along here: https://youtu.be/W0EXwE6cDAk

*We Love Ya*

*We love ya, we love ya, we love ya*

*Where you go we'll follow,*

*we'll follow, we'll follow*

*'Cuz we support the US,*

*the US, the US*

*That's the way we like it we like it,*

*we like it, we like it*

*Whooooooooooaaaooooooooooo*

# References

## Podcasts

*Best Soccer Show* with Jason Davis and Jared DuBois

*From Couva to Qatar* by The Athletic

*Full Time with Meg Linehan* by The Athletic

*State of the Union* with Alexi Lalas and David Mosse

*The Athletic Soccer Show*

## Suggested Specific Podcast Episodes

*Peter King podcast* with Dr. Celine Gounder (12-19-22)

https://tinyurl.com/2s3vfr8r

*The Daily* with Rory Smith of The New York Times on the future of soccer (12-20-22)

https://tinyurl.com/2zeu4ar5

## Written Word/Journalists

Kevin Baxter of the LA Times

Pete Pattison of The Guardian (on Qatar and human rights)

The Athletic (Felipe Cardenas, Meg Linehan, Sam Stejskal, Paul Tenorio, Steph Yang)

## Radio

Sirius XM channel 157 has Jason Davis weekday show "The United States of Soccer," and content covering U.S. Soccer. There's also a weekly USL show on Wednesdays.

## Books

"American Huckster," story on Chuck Blazer, by Mary Papenfuss and Teri Thompson

"Generation Zero," by Hal Phillips

"Making it in the Minors," by Arthur P. Solomon (baseball focused)

"Soccernomics," by Simon Kuper and Stefan Szymanski

"Star-Spangled Soccer" by Gary Hopkins

"Switching Fields," by George Dohrman

"The United States of Soccer," by Phil West

"What Happened to the USMNT: The Ugly Truth About the Beautiful Game," by Steven G. Mandis and Sarah Parsons Wolter

## Movies/TV series

*Most are for reference. A few? Pure entertainment!*

"El Presidente," Prime Video on corruption in CONMEBOL

"FIFA Uncovered," Netflix

"Good Rivals," USA vs. Mexico, Prime Video

"Kicking and Screaming," an unserious flick staring Will Ferrell on youth soccer and coffee.

"Qatar's World Cup," ESPN E60 with Jeremy Schapp

"Super League: War for Football," Apple TV

Ted Lasso," Apple TV

"The Two Escobars," ESPN 30 for 30

"Victory," This 1981 movie featured allied soccer-playing prisoners (led by Pelé, Michael Caine, and backstop Sly Stallone) defeating Nazism and sports washing.

"Welcome to Wrexham," FX and Hulu

-Websites Soccer News/History

Backheeled.com

Fourfourtwo.com

Protagonistsoccer.com

USSoccerhistory.org (Society of American Soccer History)

## Websites for Soccer Leagues

www.maslsoccer.com

www.Mlssoccer.com

www.Nisaofficial.com

www.NPSL.com

www.NWSL.com

www.USLsoccer.com

www.uwssoccer.com

www.wisleague.com

www.wpslsoccer.com

# Acknowledgments

This book would not be possible without the support of many individuals.

My "launch team" was awesome with their feedback and support. Thank you to Ben Alkaly, Bill Brady, Mark Cryan, Tom Emberly, Brian Hand, Nick Irwin, Dennis Jezek, Brian Joura, Jay Murray, Will Roleson, Bob Sutton, and Dave Walters.

Hats off to Dale R. Roberts and J.R. Heimbigner. They are two trusted online sources that help authors in the publishing process.

A few shoutouts to others who offered advice or helped include Fred Claire, a retired sports executive, and authors Mary Papenfus and Dr. Chris Yandle.

I lost three friends while writing this book. My high school friend and (American) football teammate—Rob Sorensen—and three college sports information colleagues: Lawrence Fan, Eric Moore, and Lenny Reich.

And then gut-punch of Grant Wahl's death hit during the World Cup. Our personal interaction was limited to two online messages. But Wahl showed genuine interest in reading this book. His influence on journalism and the soccer community was unmatched for his generation. Please extend a hand to someone and fight for justice in Grant's memory.

Rest in peace, brothers.

And most of all I want to thank you for reading my book!

-Bob Lowe

*I can be followed on Twitter at @robertblowe or "Author Bob Lowe" on Substack.*

Printed in Great Britain
by Amazon

21290137R00122